I Didn't
Cause It,
I Can't
Change It

How Mothers of Adult Children
with Co-occurring Disorders Have Coped

MARY RYAN WOODS
and ADRIENNE MURRAY

"I Didn't Cause It, I Can't Change It":
How Mothers of Adult Children with
Co-occurring Disorders Have Coped
By Mary Ryan Woods and Adrienne Murray

This book is not meant to substitute for proper medical diagnosis, care, or treatment related to a medical condition. Anyone deciding to make a change in care, treatment, or other routines should check with their physician.

ISBN-10: 1-942489-20-X
ISBN-13: 978-1-942489-20-7

Dedicated to RS for inspiring this book,
and to JM, whose journey has not been in vain.

Table of Contents

�kh

Foreword

No mother suspects that the birth of a child can lead to so much anguish and fear. My son was an addict starting in his teenage years. We tried dealing with it as a family by sending him to rehabs and by participating in family weeks to learn how to help him in his recovery and not be codependent. It wasn't until he was diagnosed with schizophrenia at age twenty-one that we learned about co-occurring disorders—two major mental illnesses affecting an individual simultaneously—in his case, addiction and schizophrenia.

And so the journey began to find treatment for our son and ourselves. Learning to cope with his illnesses and praying that we would find an answer for his recovery became our mission. We were never ashamed of his illnesses—we asked everyone we knew for help. We searched for programs that dealt with co-occurring disorders and found many that said they did, when in fact that was not the case. At one time he was in a mental hospital for six months and only spoke to a counselor who was trained in addiction once a week. He was in twenty-eight-day programs at several addiction rehabs where if he was lucky he saw a psychiatrist for twenty minutes a week to talk about his schizophrenia. We wanted our son back and no one was dealing with his illnesses on an equal basis. Nothing was working, and for many years he ping-ponged between hospitals and rehabs with the hope that someone could unlock the key to full recovery of both his illnesses.

He was a lost soul. There were months at a time where we had no contact with him and no idea where he was living. To this day I cannot pass up a homeless person on the street asking for money without giving them something, because I know that's how my son survived. Out of our frustration, my husband and I decided to try to create a place where men like our son could recover. Thus WestBridge was born. We thought that if we could save one family from going through the pain and suffering we had gone through, it would be worth it. We never dreamed that our son would be one of the first participants at WestBridge, but God had a plan.

As the professionals who work at WestBridge often say, it is a marathon, not a sprint! We were in this race to win, and with their help we did. I thank God every day for the recovery of our son and so many other wonderful young men who have found help and recovery at WestBridge. The journey is never completely over, but now we have a partner in his recovery.

Loralee West

Preface

ᐒ

Through the course of this book, we intend to share with you the collective experiences of twelve women who are parenting adult children with co-occurring substance use disorders and psychotic and/or affective illnesses. Our goal is for this book to be a companion and resource for those who may feel isolated and overwhelmed, coping with the same struggles these moms have lived through, so that they may find hope and wisdom.

Motherhood can come to a woman in a variety of different ways. Maybe she gave birth to her child. Maybe she became a stepmother after she married a spouse who already had children. Or perhaps she adopted her child. Regardless of how it happens, the minute a woman becomes a mother, she is acutely aware of what her child experiences. She feels her child's highs and lows.

One of the commonalities in each mother that we spoke to was the need to put her son or daughter ahead of herself. When caring for her child, the initial bond that was present when the adult child was younger seems to reengage when he or she becomes ill. The bond itself seems to be the lifeline.

Part of the journey for the mom is to eventually create a new bond that enables her to move forward with her life, thus making the mother and her adult child *interdependent* on one another.

As co-occurring mental illnesses and substance use disorders are chronic brain diseases, there is not a quick fix. Because these brain diseases are chronic in nature, often families and individuals feel treatment isn't adequate or long enough and therefore yields little or no results.

Because of the nature of these illnesses, a mother can already be exhausted after coping with a whole childhood of issues. She may have traversed the world of individualized education programs (IEPs), advocating for her child along the way. She may have felt the cruel sting of bullying as her child was singled out for being different. Her child may not have even been close to fulfilling the typical role of other children his or her age. She may have felt isolated and alone for a long period of time. Perhaps there was guilt and shame because she felt that she failed as a parent.

Other mothers may have come into this much later, after their children have been successful and grown into adulthood. Suddenly, the grown-ups that they have become look nothing like the children that they once were. No matter when the mother experiences the changes that occur because of co-occurring mental illness and substance use disorders, it is an extremely lonely and isolating time.

According to results from the 2014 National Survey on Drug Use and Health, as many as 43.6 million adults suffer from mental illness. Over 20 million adults suffer from substance use disorders. Of these numbers, 7.9 million adults suffer from co-occurring substance use disorders and mental illness. That's an average of 1 in every 30 people. Chances are, someone you know or love may suffer from these diseases. And as large as these numbers may seem, they are actually on the conservative side.[1]

Because of the way many treatment programs are designed, there are few that integrate mental illness and substance use on an equal continuum. Coupled with this, insurers and state and federal funding tend to segregate payment. There are parity laws, but there is no mandate to fund them. What all of this means is that families may have benefits but no way of accessing them. As insurance companies find ways to deny claims, individuals may have benefits but no treatment resources. Families spend hours searching for effective treatment only to find that what is advertised is not what they experience.

As with any chronic illness, no matter what that illness is, the stress and strain affects everyone in the family. Addiction has always been characterized as a family disease; it is ironic that because of the structure of most programs, the whole family does not get the treatment that is so desperately needed. Families need ongoing support to learn new coping and problem-solving skills and ways to effectively communicate with one another. These things can be achieved, but they require ongoing practice and coaching. The entire family—parents and siblings, as well as their loved one

---

[1]   Center for Behavioral Health Statistics and Quality. (2015). *Behavioral Health Trends in the United States: Results from the 2014 National Survey on Drug Use and Health* (HHS Publication No. SMA 15-4927, NSDUH Series H-50). Retrieved from http://www.samhsa.gov/ data/.

with these diseases—needs treatment. It is a disservice to those who need help the most that there are no funding streams that pay for the treatment of families standing alongside their adult children who suffer from these diseases.

Parenting a child with co-occurring mental illness and substance use disorders is a lonely and taxing journey, whether you are a mother or father. For the purposes of this book, though, we are focusing on the mother's journey. Mothers bear much of the weight of the burden of these illnesses. Emotionally, they take the brunt of the illnesses that have grabbed hold of their children. Mothers tend to be the ones who are out actively seeking resources for their children. As with everything in life, there are exceptions, but, historically speaking, the mother has the most direct contact with the child, no matter his or her stage in life. During the course of our interviews, we heard many different perspectives. The chapters that follow are a glimpse into the mother's journey.

Mary Ryan Woods

Acknowledgements

cℳɔ

As with most things in life, it takes a team of people to bring projects to fruition. I have been blessed with a wonderful team of people who contributed support, encouragement, their expertise, and, most importantly, their life experiences.

First and foremost, I want to acknowledge the fourteen women who were interviewed and whose shared experiences are the foundation of this book. They are strong, caring and amazing people from whom I have learned much.

At WestBridge Center for Integrated Treatment of Co-Occurring Disorders, we treat individuals and families who experience co-occurring mental illness and substance use disorders using integrated treatment for dual disorders and other treatments proven to work. WestBridge was created out of the experience of our founders, Loralee West and Al West, as they tried to navigate between mental health providers and addiction providers. Thank you to Dr. Robert Drake and the Dartmouth Psychiatric Research for the research they have done on co-occurring disorders which is the foundation of our programs. Often their family member "fell between the cracks" of these two systems. Their vision was to prevent other families from the experiences of nonintegrated care.

I want to acknowledge the staff at WestBridge, who go above and beyond to help our participants and families on their recovery journey. Our staff is a dedicated group of professionals who continue to model being responsive, flexible, and mobile.

I also want to acknowledge WestBridge's board of directors: Loralee West, Al West, William Doran, Frank McKee, and David Schusler, who have believed in our model of care and my vision, and without whose support neither this book nor WestBridge would be possible.

Finally, I want to thank our team of consultants, Dunleavy & Associates; my co-author, Adrienne Murray, for being patient, holding me accountable for deadlines, and contributing a writing style that is engaging and thoughtful—this project was enlightening for both of us, and I have treasured the shared experience; Patty Cook, our editor at Dunleavy, whose content and grammatical feedback was greatly appreciated; and Nancy Dunleavy, who is the epitome of "can do" and optimism, for her continued support and believing when I couldn't.

Mary Ryan Woods

◦✾◦

CHAPTER 1

The Journey

"I love the idea of a book for moms who have a child who was diagnosed with co-occurring disorders. People tend to forget that moms are affected too. In our journey, my husband and I have been huge supports for each other. We have learned so much and feel that knowledge has helped us through a lot. I would tell other mothers that there is hope and they are not alone. Just get through the storm; I promise that there is an end." —*A Mother's Perspective*

It is a universal experience for a parent to have hopes and dreams for a child starting from the very first moment the parent lays eyes on him or her. The experience of seeing a son or daughter grow is joyful in so many ways. And truly, this is no different for the parent of a son or daughter with co-occurring mental illness and substance use disorders (COD). The road for the parent of a son or daughter with COD, however, can often be lonely and isolating. What happens as a parent, specifically a mother, over the course of time realizes her adult child may not want or be able to live out the dreams the mother has held so dear?

There is almost an unwritten competition that parents have between each other. This leads to the shame that a mother may feel, isolating her even further and preventing her from seeking the help that she and her family so desperately need. Collectively, society says, "We know that not everyone can be the head cheerleader or the captain of the football team," but perhaps there's a secret, unspoken desire that all parents harbor: "They can't all be, but maybe, just maybe, my son or daughter will be the *one*."

The depth of emotions that mothers experience in their journey to healing is very different from the experience of other caretakers or family members. It is a unique journey for every man, woman, and son or daughter. Perhaps you wonder if anyone makes it through this roller coaster journey unscathed. The answer is no. But that doesn't mean that the family and the person with COD cannot heal. Healing can happen, and when it does, it is a beautiful thing.

The journey for each of these moms is fraught with so many emotions and painful realities. It might begin early in her child's life. And then again, maybe not; co-occurring disorders have no respect for time, and the journey can start at any point in a person's life. Ultimately, as harsh as it may sound, the parent must accept that he or she will always have a child with co-occurring disorders. And as important as it is to find the right treatment for the son or daughter, it is just as important for a mom to get treatment for herself as soon as possible so that she can begin her own journey to recovery.

As any mother knows, the mom wears many hats and plays many roles. For the mother of a son or daughter with COD, the role of first responder is one that she knows well. If her child manifested mental illness at a young age, then she was the one who got the call from school. She was expected to deal more punishment at home because her son or daughter wouldn't sit still in class. The moms that we interviewed were quite unanimous in saying that when their children found the right treatment, and they were no longer in the role of first responder, it gave them the ability to step back for a moment and come to terms with the reality of their situations.

The pain that a mother feels for her child who clearly does not feel like he or she fits in seems almost too much to bear. When an elementary-school-aged child hangs a sign on his or her bedroom door with a face drawn with only a straight line for a smile and simply entitles the work "Mr. Nobody," how can a mother's own heart not break? Not only can she feel her son or daughter's pain, but also this taps into the humanity that we all share. Who, at some point in his or her own life, has not felt like a nobody?

And so a mother, strapped into the seat of the roller coaster by the circumstances of having a son or daughter with COD, starts creeping up the first hill. She waits to get to the top of the track, not knowing what awaits her over the crest. It is terrifying, but just like on an amusement park roller coaster, there is no way to make the operator stop and let you off before the ride is over. Imagine the guilt a mother feels because she may even dare to want to get off of the roller coaster.

In the beginning, this first responder can be told by doctors, teachers, and television—all of society, really—that she is held responsible for her son or daughter's seemingly defiant refusal to fit into societal norms. Believing what she has been told, the mother takes it upon herself to fix the problem. She feels, in effect, that it's all her fault. Historically speaking, women have been the sole caretakers for the children in the family. The son or daughter, being the mother's responsibility, becomes a reflection of her ability to mother. No wonder her identity becomes wrapped up in the perceived successes and failures of her son or daughter.

Not that long ago, it was thought that one of the causes of schizophrenia was what psychiatrist Theodore Lidz labeled the "schizophrenogenic mother."[2] In his books *Schizophrenia and the Family* and *The Origin and Treatment of Schizophrenic Disorders*, Lidz points to research he conducted with families of children with schizophrenia. He asserted that when one spouse (the mother) is domineering while the other (the father) is passive, the domineering spouse can push a distorted view of the world on the family, thus confining her family into narrow limits that she could easily control and presumably "creating" a schizophrenic son or daughter.

Lidz later wrote that he found it "very distressing that because the parents' attitudes and interactions are important determinants of schizophrenic disorders, some therapists and

---

[2]   See Glossary for definition of the schizophrenogenic mother

family caseworkers treat parents as villains who have ruined the lives of their patients." Unfortunately for many parents, mothers in particular, the damage was already done. She was seen as the problem rather than part of the solution. A textbook written by Lidz, *The Person*, which asserts the misguided concept that a parent can cause schizophrenia, has been used in many areas of higher learning.

Imagine how many women have been told that because they may be outspoken and their husband more laid back that they created the schizophrenia that has taken hold of their child. Now consider the women who are prone to anxiety. It is our experience that these women have been told by well-meaning people that if they weren't so anxious, their son or daughter wouldn't be either. As with everything, perhaps there is a grain of truth. But there is a mound of research that backs up the fact that we cannot create COD just because of the way we parent. If your parenting style didn't create it, how can anyone expect your parenting style to heal it?

What we do know is that genetics, epigenetics, diet, exposure to toxins, and more all contribute to COD. There is *no* known single cause. Treating something that you cannot see with methods that may or may not work is scary. Even when parents can, without a doubt in their minds, point to a genetic reason for a malady, they can feel guilt and shame for not being able to make their sons or daughters healthy. Guilt is just part of the package with parenting any child. Shame enters in when the mother feels that she or her child isn't measuring up to the community standard as a result of her inadequacy.

Characteristically, the journey that a mother of an adult child with COD takes can manifest in isolation, shame, and guilt. The stress of not knowing where to turn for help could be enough to break anyone. All parents feel the strain of trying to help their children maximize their potential. Parents with children who have COD don't feel this any less. Coupled with that, sometimes they are in a life-and-death struggle, just trying to keep their son or daughter alive. The moms that we talked to stressed that they had to adjust how they measured success.

Under the healthiest of conditions, raising a son or daughter is not an easy task. How much more powerless the parent of a child with an illness must feel. There is no manual, and even knowing the right questions to ask is difficult. You don't know what you don't know. Until a stage of acceptance of the diagnosis is reached, a mother can struggle with a great deal of grief. Finally coming to a point where the mother decides that she is going to continue living her life, whether her son or daughter survives or not, is a weighty burden to shoulder.

The burdens that a mother must shoulder become even heavier because of the emotions involved. One of the easiest go-to emotions is anger. Anger that her son or daughter is different, anger at his or her behavior, anger even that the child is not fulfilling her dreams. Anger at treatment, anger at her partner for not doing enough. Maybe even anger at her partner for doing too much for an adult son or daughter. Anger at the world for not understanding. Truly, as one of the moms that we interviewed said, "It's easier to be mad than sad."

We all have things that, if we let them, keep us up at night. The mind is where a huge part of this emotional roller coaster of a journey takes place. Fearful images play over and over again in the mind's eye. Fear of death. Fear of the abusive behaviors a once sweet son or daughter is now exhibiting. For the mother of a person with COD, the sight of her adult child looking unclean and disheveled is one such image. The smell that tells her he or she has been using substances stays in her nose for longer than the physical smell that permeates her son or daughter's clothing. The look in her child's eyes that says the son or daughter that she packed a lunch for and sent off for the first day of kindergarten is no longer there. The struggle of not knowing where her child is. The struggle of knowing where her child is but not knowing what choices he or she is making.

One of the moms whom we interviewed told us that as she progressed in her own journey of healing, being able to actually feel the fear was a sign of her own strength. You see, to dull her emotions and hold the fear at bay, she medicated herself. And it helped her through the most difficult time of her life. But there came a time when she didn't need the medication anymore, and she celebrated her independence. She celebrated her small steps just as she celebrated her child's.

A mother can often go through a great deal of denial about her child's illness. For a mother whose child developed typically, and so his or her diseases weren't discovered until later in life, the diagnosis is a bitter pill to swallow indeed. She feels like what is happening to her son or daughter is just a blip, and that what's happening within her family really isn't that bad. She reasons that her son or daughter will grow out of this stage and will be who they once were again. For some children this is true, while for others it is not.

For the parent of a son or daughter with COD, the sting of seeing the adult children of neighbors, friends, and other family members moving forward with their lives hurts. When the mother of a person with COD celebrates success, such as her grown child wearing clean clothes without any prompting, it is truly no less amazing than when the neighbor's child goes off to an Ivy League college. Unfortunately, society as a whole does not see the same value. The yardstick that the mother of a person with COD uses to measure success becomes far different that it may have been even a few years earlier.

What a very lonely and isolating place to be. Some moms stop talking and don't join in conversations anymore, isolating themselves and in turn feeling isolated by others. Perhaps it's out of fear that they will be asked how their son or daughter is doing. Perhaps it's just because they are exhausted and are moving through the day, going through the motions in a daze. Considering this, it's no wonder that some mothers say that they are only as happy as their least happy child.

This journey, with all of its high and lows, is as much about the mother as it is about the individual with the diseases. A mother must learn how to support her son or daughter but have a life of her own. More often than not, there are other family members that she is responsible for as well. The complexity of her role is staggering. Often her relationship with her other children is affected, and they may feel the need to take care of her, or they may feel abandoned by her for the needs of their sibling.

When the isolation ends and shame, guilt, and fear are no longer given room to exist, families really can heal. It takes a long time, as these illnesses are not acute but are chronic in nature. As one mother put it, "When you remember that you really know the essence of your son or daughter, it gives you hope. And that seed of hope, no matter how tiny it may be, is the promise of the healing that is to come."

There are so many supports out there for families as well as individuals with COD. One such organization is the National Alliance on Mental Illness (NAMI). It is the nation's largest grassroots mental health organization dedicated to helping the millions of Americans affected by mental illness. Or Al-Anon, an organization that helps friends and families of people who abuse substances find support and understanding. Celebrate Recovery is a Christ-centered recovery program that is now being used in thousands of churches nationwide. In addition to these supports, many treatment centers have parents' groups or alumni groups that can be a source of support.

Among the mothers we interviewed, we found that the saying rings true, "There are no atheists in a foxhole." Whether the mother started her journey with faith in a higher power or not, she certainly came to believe that the spiritual life is not a just theory. Faith and prayer were common coping tools for the moms that we interviewed. Being able to turn their fears and frustrations over to the God of their understanding sustained many of them through the difficult times on their journeys.

When a mother gets to the point that she is able to share her journey with others, healing can begin to take place. Reacting to situations in faith instead of fear is a benchmark of her growth. The outcome of her child's illnesses will only be known over the course of time; the experiences of the moms who contributed to this vary from suicide to continued illness and finally to recovery. The journey that a mother is on differs from that of her son or daughter. And though the days may seem dark, where there is hope, there is light. And, true to the nature of light, it dispels the darkness.

Al-Anon Three Cs
I didn't Cause it, I can't Control it, I can't Cure it

CHAPTER 2

The Emotional Roller Coaster

"I remember, in the beginning, I felt like I was in a daze. Looking back, I was just trying to get through the day, I suppose. Since then, though, education has been key for me. I'm surprised to hear that other mothers were blamed for their children's illnesses. As for feeling isolated, this certainly did happen to me. But my friends and family have come out of the darkness about mental illness and their support has helped more than I can say." —A Mother's Perspective

When a parent instructs a younger child, it is hands-on and directive: "Did you look both ways when you crossed the street?" An answer of yes gets a nod of approval, while a no means that a child needs further instruction. The expectations were clear about what the child needed to do to learn to be safe and happy. When the child is young, "right and wrong" and parenting are so easy compared to adolescence and beyond when the son or daughter has co-occurring disorders. As an individual grows through adolescence and into adulthood, it is very natural for the questions and parenting skills to change: Were there drugs at the party? Did my child take any? How do I support my son's anxiety? How do I cope with my daughter's mania?

Now consider a mother, who already feels shame that she cannot protect her child from the voices in his or her head or the consequences of drinking too much or taking drugs, and how powerless she must feel to the pull of the substance that has a vice-like grip on her son or daughter. The questions are different for this mother. They are more urgent, and the answers could mean life or death: Where were you? How much did you take? What is wrong with you? Who can help us?

With co-occurring disorders, life becomes a series of ups and downs. When someone climbs into the seat of a roller coaster willingly, he or she has, in effect, allowed another to control his or her fate and is able to get off at the end of the ride. However, the mother of an individual with COD did not choose to sit in this roller coaster and feels powerless to get off and stop the process. Her fate is no longer in her own hands but has been given over to a disease that she can't see and doesn't know how to heal. These emotions are certainly debilitating in the beginning, as the mother struggles to find the accurate diagnosis and treatment for her child.

The first hill on this roller coaster may be when she first sees results of the symptoms and behaviors her son or daughter is experiencing. A mother, knowing her child better than most anyone and having the role of first responder, often is the first to see that something may not be right. Perhaps she tries to convince herself that this is just a phase. Well-meaning friends and even medical providers may perpetuate this belief, saying that all kids find themselves and that her child will work it out on his or her own. While this may be true in many cases, it is not for that of a person with co-occurring disorders.

A mother may even surprise herself with her reactions. Perhaps a mother who jumped to action to pull her toddler away from a hot stove before it could be touched struggles later in life when she is told to take a step back and let her child fail on his or her own. Or maybe a mother was laid back when her child scraped a knee falling off of a bike, only to rage against school officials when they dare question where the youth was during school hours, though she knows full well that her child was not with her or anywhere that he or she was supposed to be.

Of the mothers we spoke with, many say that they experienced a lack of trust in themselves and the belief that they could deal with the situation. They each felt they couldn't trust their son or daughter because of the behaviors exhibited. And they couldn't trust the treatment providers because they felt that the providers didn't listen. Some were angry with God—Why is God doing this to us? Why are we being punished?—while others asserted that without God, they wouldn't get through it.

Nagging, utter fear, even when parents accept what they've been told, has contributed to many sleepless nights for parents of children with COD. The sad fact is that many health care providers know so little about COD. Not only is it difficult for many to make a diagnosis, when a diagnosis is finally reached, few providers know where to refer their patients for treatment.

Seeing a person's personality change and the associated behaviors, such as paranoid delusions and disinhibition, along with other behaviors that happen under the influence, can be scary. A mother often has a great deal of fear for the individual's safety as well as her own. These diseases are at the root of some real life-and-death situations. People with COD may harm themselves intentionally or unintentionally. And they can often become the target of others, singled out for behaviors that look so different from those around them.

One of the greatest fears a mother has is of not being able to do anything to help. This fear seems founded, given the variety of treatment experiences to which individuals are subjected. The mother knows her son or daughter, but everyone else may see the child very differently. This roller coaster affects the relationship, taking its toll on everyone involved. It is not just the individual with COD who suffers; the family suffers as well. Mothers sometimes can't help but feel guilt for taking themselves away from their other children and their partner as they turn their focus to the son or daughter with COD.

Many mothers are in disbelief about the diagnosis of COD. And until they come to terms with the fact that there is no magic bullet for these chronic brain diseases, it is normal for a mother to feel frustration and anger. Anger is felt because things aren't getting better quickly or their son or daughter isn't doing enough to get better. A mother may feel angry that it's not in her power to make the change for her son or daughter who is, at this moment, so powerless against these diseases.

As with many other struggles in life, financial worries can be a substantial part of this roller coaster. Financial worries are significant for moms if they have to take time off from work and there is a loss of income. In many instances, insurance won't cover the treatment that is deemed most effective, and families go into debt to pay for treatment. Other parents may experience guilt and remorse for not being able to provide the treatment that may work but that they cannot afford. More worries take hold as mothers wonder how they can continue supporting their children as they themselves get older and leave the work force.

A mother may grieve the life she thought she was going to have with her son or daughter. Maybe she worked harder than she ever thought she could so that she could put him or her through medical school, only to find that the promise the individual showed was stymied by the growth of these diseases. There is a sense of loss when a mother realizes that the hopes she had for her child will never be attained and even developmental milestones are in question due to these chronic brain diseases.

It can take several years of good treatment for an individual to begin to understand the toll COD can take. The moms that we interviewed found that the grieving changes over time, and as their loved ones enter into recovery, the grief changes and begins to fade. Grief and depression are two completely different things. A mother will experience grief in layers, and when she can learn to overcome guilt, she can come to a place where she gives herself permission to grieve. When a mother learns to enjoy a good day for what it is, healing for her own frazzled emotions can occur.

The diagnosis of co-occurring disorders does not have to ensure a lifetime of dark days for the family or the individual. We know that with the right treatment, resources, and community supports, a person living with COD can go on to live a full and productive life. But for some individuals, this is not the case. What happens when things go terribly wrong, and a life is taken by these diseases? Even with the best of care and intentions, the outcome of these diseases can be devastating. Individuals can become victims of violence, significant trauma, or mental or sexual abuse. They are more susceptible to early onset medical diseases and are even at risk for suicide. Though energy, family resources, effort, and time may have been put into recovery, there are no guarantees that anything is going to work. The realization that sacrifices were made in vain for shared dreams can create a profound sense of grief.

Trauma, diminished self-image, and the constant feeling of failure by both the family and individual can cause a person to take his or her own life. Because of the myths that surround mental illness and addiction, rejection can come from many areas, including society, church, and the criminal justice system. For many families, this is the reality. How do they keep moving forward when, in fact, they find that there is no magic fix? In the end, for some, all of this can prove to be too much to overcome. This is a very painful journey for the individual as well as the family. It is vital for a mother who has experienced the death of her son or daughter to find support and treatment for herself. This is a path that no one should walk alone and has unfortunately been well trodden by many others.

When it comes to understanding chronic brain diseases, education is key. People recover slowly over time. Since these diseases are chronic in nature, it is vital to understand that there is no quick fix to a chronic condition. If the treatment doesn't seem to be working or doesn't meet expectations, families can educate themselves and find what has worked for others in their situation. Talking on an emotional level with others who have lived through this roller coaster can be key in finding an answer. And just as the individual with the COD benefits from having a good mentor, so does the parent.

To make it through the roller coaster of emotions, the mother needs to find what works best for her. For some mothers, work is an antidote. For others, it may be artwork, exercise, or meditation—any number of things, really. The NAMI Family-to-Family program, Al-Anon, and faith groups are a place of solace, education, and support. If grief gives way to depression or other mental illness, the mother needs to find a healthcare provider to take care of her own needs.

The act of mothering comes with so many emotions in and of itself. No matter the age of a child, when he or she struggles, the mother feels those struggles as well. Every parent looks back and says, "If only I had…" But that way of thinking needs to be put to rest, especially when a mother is parenting an individual with COD. Remember that small victories need to be celebrated as heartily as the large ones.

Kübler-Ross's Five Stages of Grief[3]
Denial, Anger, Bargaining, Depression, Acceptance

---

[3]   Elizabeth Kübler-Ross and David Kessler, *On Grief and Grieving: Finding the Meaning of Grief Through the Five Stages of Loss* (New York: Scribner, 2007).

∿

CHAPTER 3

Shame, Secrecy, and Stigma

"I spent a lot of time wondering what I didn't do right as a parent. Truth be told, I still have those days. But what I know now is that this is a lifelong illness, and recovery can be slow. But there is recovery. As for the stigma surrounding co-occurring disorders? I've learned that when people speak out, the stigma is broken." —A Mother's Perspective

"After over nine years, there are so many things I have been able to put to rest in my head, and for that I am grateful. When I look back, I see that I used the wrong yardstick to measure the successes and failures of my child. As time has gone on, I have become more vocal when I see stigma and prejudice. My journey was isolated, and I did not have many supports. I tried NAMI, but it was almost too much for me to bear, to hear all of the stories of other families, although I have gotten a lot out of a family-to-family class I have been a part of. Honestly, for me, work has been a place in which I have found respite." —A Mother's Perspective

Our society, no matter how accepting it is in some ways, can be very intolerant of people with differences. Media in general plays no small role in perpetuating this intolerance and prejudice. Whether on the news, where reporters play amateur psychiatrist, or on television stations that air programs depicting people with mental illnesses in a negative light, misinformation is pushed upon us all. The headlines and TV shows, among other things, often pair mental illnesses and substance use disorders with violence. In effect, this creates an "us and them" atmosphere.

Take the myth that people with mental illnesses are more prone to violence. In fact, according to the US Department of Health and Human Services, only 3 to 5 percent of violent acts are attributed to people living with mental illness. And they are over *ten times* more likely to be victims of a violent crime.[4] Behaviors that someone with COD may exhibit might look frightening or different, but it is preposterous to assume just because of the behavior that anyone will be harmed.

Imagine what this societal influence does to a mother when she first hears the diagnosis of obsessive-compulsive disorder, schizophrenia, alcoholism, heroin addiction, or any other number of mental illnesses. How different it must be for her than for a mother who hears that her child has cancer. Cancer is a disease that our society has invested large sums of money in to find a cure. We have accepted that cancer requires multiple episodes of treatment. However, when a person is diagnosed with schizophrenia, alcoholism, or other related diseases, the *person* seems to be the object of scorn and

---

4   "Mental Health Myths and Facts," MentalHealth.gov, accessed March 4, 2016, http://www.mentalhealth.gov/basics/myths-facts/.

not the *disease*.

Many of the mothers we interviewed said that one of the things that hurt them the most was when their own family members lost sight of who their child really was. They seemed to only focus on the symptoms and behaviors related to the co-occurring disorders and often forgot about the true nature of that individual. Some felt as if friends, family, the medical community, and even strangers blamed their parenting for their child's diseases. Imagine the public outcry if the parents of a child with cancer were blamed for their child's illness.

Some mothers may lose friendships because of prevailing stigma. Stigma can turn a word of genuine concern into an ugly and hurtful dart that pierces right through a mothers' protective armor and into her heart. When a mother is asked if she is afraid for her life because of the behaviors brought about by co-occurring disorders and exhibited by her adult child, it makes her unwilling to share her experience with anyone else. When friends respond with fear and prejudice instead of empathy and understanding, the mother is driven further into shame and guilt.

Part of the stigma surrounding COD that causes so much isolation is the idea that the manifestations of the disease are simply a matter of will power that can be overcome. Because of misconceptions around the different diagnostic labels, people believe a number of things that are incorrect about co-occurring disorders. For instance, many people believe that schizophrenia is split personality. The rare diagnosis of multiple personalities is very different from schizophrenia. Schizophrenia, which is characterized as being split off from reality, is not so rare and affects an estimated 1 in 100 people.[5]

There are many things that have to come together for COD to happen. The debate goes on, and the scientific community is not unanimous on what, if any, are the contributing factors that create these diseases. Where one person may be resilient, another may not be. For instance, two children from one abusive household are likely to walk away with differing degrees of trauma. The fact is that some people are more resilient while others are more susceptible to co-occurring disorders.

According to the Centers for Disease Control and Prevention, mental illness is a health condition that is characterized by altered thinking, mood, or behavior. An article written by Kristen Weir for the American Psychological Association reports that there is currently a general shift, and people now tend to view mental illness disorders as brain diseases. [6] However, prejudice dies hard, and even though people are better educated about brain diseases, common thoughts and reactions in society have not caught up with science. In regards to addiction, scientific research shows that it is a disease that affects the brain and the behavior of an individual.[7] In short, exposure to a substance may activate the genetic component linked to these brain diseases.

[5]   "Schizophrenia: Symptoms, Types, Causes, and Early Warning Signs," HelpGuide.org, last modified February 2016, http://www.helpguide.org/articles/schizophrenia/schizophrenia-signs-types-and-causes.htm.

[6]   Kristen Weir, "The Roots of Mental Illness: How Much of Mental Illness Can the Biology of the Brain Explain?" *Monitor on Psychology* 43 no.6 (June 2012): 30, accessed March 4, 2016, http://www.apa.org/monitor/2012/06/roots.aspx.

[7]   "DrugFacts: Understanding Drug Abuse and Addiction," National Institute on Drug Abuse, last modified November 2012, https://www.drugabuse.gov/publications/drugfacts/ understanding-drug-abuse-addiction.

One thing that can come as a surprise to many parents who have children in varying stages of drug use is that even casual drug use can lead to addiction. According to Alan I. Leshner, PhD, the former director of the National Institute of Drug Abuse, National Institutes of Health, once the brain becomes accustomed to the euphoria that the drug brings, the brain begins to demand that substance. Repeated use changes the function and structure of the brain, and what begins as voluntary usage becomes compulsory. The way that the brain changes can vary with each person who uses. The impact can be long-lasting biochemical makeup changes, brain or mood changes, or memory and motor skills loss. Dr. Leshner calls this the "oops phenomenon." No one intentionally sets out to become an ardent drug user. But sometimes when biology and behavior combine, this is exactly what occurs.[8]

All of these common misconceptions can result in a culture that blames a parent, causing guilt, isolation, and embarrassment. And truly, these are just a few of the negative results that can cause a mother to withdraw and not seek help.

The natural instinct of a mother is to protect her child. How difficult it must be for a mother who thinks that perhaps she caused her child's drug use, anxiety, or what society perceives as bizarre behavior. A mother may be told that her anxiety caused her child to be anxious. Or perhaps she's told that her status as a single parent didn't provide her child a strong enough role model, and so her child found that role model elsewhere. She is told, in effect, what she's done

---

[8]   Alan I. Leshner, "Oops: How Casual Drug Use Leads to Addiction," accessed March 4, 2016, http://archives.drugabuse.gov/Published_Articles/Oops.html.

or is doing isn't good enough. And not only is it not good enough, she caused this damage to the one she was supposed to safeguard.

So the mother goes inward. Friends become afraid to ask how things are going. And if they do ask, they never get into details. A mother can say that she doesn't care what others think. But in reality, she may; it can be painful living in a society that oftentimes villainizes her son or daughter.

Embarrassment comes when a grown child does not live up to or fulfill the role the parents or community sees him or her in. "Johnny has always been good at sports and now all he cares about is getting high. What a *waste*. What a *loser*. What is *wrong* with his parents that they *let* him do that?" Or, "Jenny was always so smart and pretty. Have you *seen* how she looks? Did you *hear* what she did? *Where* are her parents? What a *shame*."

Good parenting develops good kids, right? If you do everything the right way, everything will be fine, right? Not always. There are extreme situations, but remember Al-Anon's three Cs: You didn't **C**ause it, you can't **C**ontrol it, and you can't **C**ure it.

What we found is that the biggest combatant to this stigma and shame is the voice of the mother. When mothers begin to step up and speak out, amazing things can happen. Coming full circle, friends who were once afraid to "get into things" call for advice. These same mothers, who may have felt paralyzed by embarrassment and shame, act as a bridge between two worlds. Educating their families and friends about the realities of co-occurring disorders, the moms are quietly and not so quietly changing the way we think about these diseases.

"Stigma is a process by which the reaction of others spoils normal identity." —Erving Goffman

"Mental illness is nothing to be ashamed of, but stigma and bias shame us all." —Bill Clinton

❧

CHAPTER 4

Experience of Treatment

"I was obsessed with finding a solution for my child's illness. In hindsight, I probably wasted too much time trying to be the perfect parent, not realizing that this disease didn't have anything to do with my parenting. Praying has helped me come to terms with things, as has the empathy my pastor's had for my family. I'm still in the process of learning and don't have all of the answers. Education and support groups such as Al-Anon and NAMI are key, though." —A Mother's Perspective

"I felt so unprepared but found education to be the key in this journey. And other moms who are going through this need to remember to take care of themselves. Don't isolate yourself, and find support from others who have gone on this same journey. Now, I share with friends and meditate. These tools have proven to be a huge help to me." —A Mother's Perspective

Treatment comes in many forms, such as inpatient, outpatient, supported housing, and web-based counseling. It is important for families to look for treatment that is integrated, includes families, and is based on the Stages of Change model.[9] The most effective treatment is person centered rather than having the individual fit the program. As is true for all chronic illnesses, there needs to be a continuum of care that supports the individual and family over the course of acuity and recovery.

When looking at treatment for co-occurring mental illness and substance use disorders, families need to find integrated treatment for dual disorders, which is an evidence-based practice. Integrated treatment for dual disorders is a model of treatment that identifies both mental illness and substance use disorders as primary illnesses requiring treatment at the *same* time by the *same* treatment team in the *same* location. The treatment team is a multidiscipline team that provides treatment, case management, and community support.

There are other models of treatment, which research has shown to be very ineffective:

- A single model of treatment—designed to identify one disorder as primary. The thought is that once the person's substance use disorder or mental illness is treated effectively, the other disorder will resolve itself.

- A sequential model of treatment—identifies both co-occurring illnesses, but one is deemed primary and treated first. Upon stabilization of the primary illness, the other disorder is treated.

---

[9]   Please see model in Appendix B.

- A parallel model of treatment— identifies both the mental illness and substance use disorder, and treatment is provided by separate treatment teams and often in separate treatment centers, with little coordination of treatment or record sharing.[10]

Quadrants of Care[10]

	Substance use severity		
high		III high substance use severity and low mental health disorder(s) severity	IV high substance use severity and high mental health disorder(s) severity
low		I low substance use severity and low mental health disorder(s) severity	II low substance use severity and high mental health disorder(s) severity
		low Mental health disorder(s) severity high	

There are many "doors" to treatment that families may enter. At a program such as the one at WestBridge, the treatment system is set up to respond to different levels of acuity and intensity as outlined in the following chart.

Treatment in quadrant I typically occurs with a primary care physician, quadrant II in a mental health clinic, quadrant III in an addiction treatment setting, and quadrant IV in a specialized treatment setting that provides integrated treatment for dual disorders. Finding the treatment setting that best meets the needs of the family member requires consumer education and sometimes a consumer advocate.

Diagnosis and treatment are yet another stage in this journey. Often a mother has always known her son or daughter was not developing normally. In other cases, the mother may have felt that a behavior change came out of left field. No matter if co-occurring diseases were a struggle for years or came

---

10   "A Guide to Substance Abuse Services for Primary Care Clinicians," Center for Substance Abuse Treatment, accessed March 4, 2016, http://store.samhsa.gov/product/TIP-24-Guide-to-Substance-Abuse-Services-for-Primary-Care-Clinicians/SMA08-4075.

on suddenly, the diagnosis can be a hard truth for any parent.

Imagine the mother who is exhausted after years of advocating for her child. She is no stranger to the labels that society has for her son or daughter and perhaps welcomes a diagnosis. Perhaps she feels that a diagnosis is the light at the end of the very long tunnel she has been traveling through. A name means she may be able to help her loved one reach the potential that she has seen all along.

Consider now the mother who has been able to see her child reach his or her potential as he or she developed and matured. Her child excelled at sports or school or making friends. Suddenly, though, it's as if a stranger has taken over, and the mother feels blindsided by what is happening with her child. All of the dreams she may have held dear are seemingly gone when she hears a diagnosis that she may not understand and that she has only heard whispered about from the shadows. Or perhaps she has a family history and had hoped against hope that her offspring would not fall prey to the same diagnosis.

Finding a diagnosis can be very hard, and families are often given one diagnosis after another. It is terrifying to families when "experts" can't even agree. When the people they've turned to for help seem to be taking shots in the dark. And when they do land on a diagnosis, this can be equally as terrifying. Many mothers we talked to expressed how very difficult it was to accept the diagnosis their children had been given. Oftentimes it is an enormous struggle for a mother to come to terms with what the diagnosis means for her child's future.

In the late 1960s, a man named Bill Milliken wrote a book called *Tough Love* that promoted authoritarian parenting. Mr. Milliken is best known as an advocate for disenfranchised youth, and his work helped many young people succeed where they may not have before. So it was, when the culture of "tough love" parenting was born, many parents thought this was the magic bullet for their children.

Sadly, since co-occurring disorders are chronic brain diseases, this form of parenting has hurt more than it has helped those with COD. Mothers were told to do what was in direct opposition to their natural instincts. They were called "helicopter parents." They were told that their children weren't getting better because they wouldn't let go and let their loved ones figure things out on their own. Contrary to the idea of tough love, the support of a united family unit, the definition of which changes from family to family, is the best indicator of success for an individual with COD.

As a parent continues on the journey with a son or daughter who has co-occurring disorders, one of the most complicated and frustrating components can be finding the right treatment facility. Co-occurring disorders are much different from the stand-alone diagnosis of mental illness or substance use. If a person with COD receives treatment for a mental illness and the substance use is not addressed, any ground that is gained against the disease may soon be lost. And the same is true for a facility that treats only substance use and neglects the mental illness diagnosis.

The term "co-occurring disorders" is commonly used to describe any two coexisting conditions, such as diabetes and hypertension, or depression and alcohol abuse. Many treatment facilities market treating co-occurring disorders, and it is essential for the individual and/or family to identify which illnesses the facility has experience in treating. Sometimes advertisements are misleading, and it is vital to be an informed consumer.

Even when a person is severely symptomatic, it can be exceedingly difficult without the individual's consent to get him or her into treatment. It oftentimes takes a major incident, such as a hospitalization or arrest, to have a person admitted for treatment. When hospitalization does occur, because of insurance constraints or due to the method of treatment, individuals are far too often sent home before any real work can begin. Often, treatment does not include the family or provide the family the skills needed to navigate the transition to home. And when the individual does go home, many times a family is paralyzed by the behaviors that are manifested. Where can they turn?

As you will see in the chart below, there are many different types of treatment for co-occurring disorders: integrated treatment for dual disorders, assertive community treatment (ACT), supported employment, family therapy, motivational interviewing, and twelve-step programs, to name a few. Whatever treatment is chosen for COD, the mental illness and substance use aspect must be treated concurrently.[11]

---

[11]   Adapted from Kim Muser et al., *Integrated Treatment for Dual Disorders: A Guide to Effective Practice* (New York: The Guilford Press, 2003).

Addiction Treatment	Mental Health Treatment	Integrated Treatment
Peer counselor model that evolved to include professionals	Medical/ professional model that evolved to include peers	Originally designed to include both peers and professionals
Based on spiritual recovery and abstinence	Utilizes scientific treatment with little focus on spirituality	Combines and integrates the principles of addiction treatment with scientific treatment
Twelve-step based	Medication based	Integrates twelve-step, mutual support, medication, and other evidence-based practices
Uses confrontation and expectation	Provides support and flexibility	Integrates expectation, support, flexibility, and hope

Addiction Treatment	Mental Health Treatment	Integrated Treatment
Detachment/ empowerment	Case management/care	Empowerment, relational, responsive, case management
Episodic treatment	Continuous treatment	Continuous treatment using assertive case management
Recovery ideology	Deinstitutionalizati on ideology	Recovery ideology
Views mental illness as secondary to addiction	Views addiction as secondary to mental illness	Views both addiction and mental illness as primary, occurring in the brain at the same time
Views relationships as a vehicle for recovery	Views relationships as a source of transference and countertransference	Views relationships as a vehicle for recovery

Addiction Treatment	Mental Health Treatment	Integrated Treatment
Views addiction as a disease that affects the whole family, and therefore the family needs treatment	Views mental illness as more of an individual illness	Views diseases as affecting the whole family, and therefore the family needs treatment

By the time a family finally finds effective treatment, it may have been through many different providers who used a variety of different treatment methods. For many mothers, it is hard when their children go into treatment and they suddenly find themselves on the outside. They may feel that they no longer really know what's going on, especially when providers begin to switch labels, and the initial diagnosis is deemed wrong.

When a mother entrusts her child to the care of a provider because he or she needs treatment, it can be hard to trust the process. She may feel that she is completely shut out. Worse yet, she may have been shamed or blamed by the provider, who told her she was at fault and should step out and let the professionals do their jobs. Treatment can, in effect, become more challenging than helpful.

Another component to finding treatment is trying to access insurance benefits. Mothers may feel that in the process of advocating for their children, they spend more hours sitting in a waiting room while providers undertake the task of working with insurance companies. Even though more awareness is being raised that co-occurring disorders are chronic brain diseases, insurance companies are very slow to change the way they reimburse for treatment. Providers everywhere are hopeful that this will change in the near future. Until then, the sad fact is that insurance companies only pay for acute care for this chronic condition.

There are parity laws, which were created to protect the consumer. As explained by the US Department of Labor, "the Mental Health Parity and Addiction Equity Act of 2008 (MHPAEA) requires group health plans and health insurance issuers to ensure that financial requirements (such as co-pays, deductibles) and treatment limitations (such as visit limits) applicable to mental health or substance use disorder (MH/SUD) benefits are no more restrictive than the predominant requirements or limitations applied to substantially all medical/surgical benefits. MHPAEA supplements prior provisions under the Mental Health Parity Act of 1996 (MHPA), which required parity with respect to aggregate lifetime and annual dollar limits for mental health benefits."[12]

Unfortunately, these laws are either not enforced or are only partially enforced. What this means is that payment is often only remitted when the insured person holds the insurance companies responsible. All of this takes education, time, and energy. For those who are already weary from the effects these diseases have had on their families, this proves to be a very heavy burden to shoulder.

---

[12] "Mental Health Parity," United States Department of Labor, Employee Benefits Security Administration, accessed March 4, 2016, http://www.dol.gov/ebsa/mentalhealthparity/.

When a family makes it over the financial mountain it must climb, there is still no guarantee of the success of its efforts. How difficult it must be when the family feels that they have found the right treatment, doctor, and medication, only to have things go awry. Often the initial episode of treatment doesn't yield the results they had been hoping for, or finding the right medication takes more precious time. In addition to this, some treatment approaches abruptly discharge the individual from treatment after they have a relapse with alcohol use or an exacerbation of the mental illness becomes apparent. For a parent, these all add up and may seem like more failures. The roller coaster ride continues with no apparent end in sight.

What the family of a loved one with co-occurring disorders needs to understand is that with these chronic diseases, setbacks can and do occur. And in an effective treatment program for an individual with co-occurring disorders, every setback is an opportunity for growth. Even if a prognosis looks bleak, never give up. Reconciliation and recovery can be around the corner. It may just take longer to get there than the family first hoped.

Another common obstacle in treatment is when an individual who has experienced psychotic or manic episodes presents well while in treatment but not when he or she is in the home environment. This can be frustrating for families and providers alike. The reality is that these types of brain diseases are incredibly individual. It takes the patience of the family paired with a provider who has proven outcomes to create lasting change and recovery.

The beauty and the hope of healing is that for people with COD, there is a 50 percent decrease of hospitalization over time if they have adequate family supports in place. The importance of ongoing family involvement in treatment is key to an individual's future success. There is a continued need for families to develop new skills in communication and problem solving. The education of the entire family is paramount to the success of the individual with these chronic brain diseases.

CHAPTER 5

When Things Go Wrong

"Through all of this, I have learned a lot about myself. I thought I was a strong person, but I had never had anything test my limits. I've learned to put aside the things I cannot change or influence and focus on what I can. I would tell other mothers to take this journey one day at a time."
—A Mother's Perspective

For an individual with co-occurring disorders, the sad truth is that when things go wrong, they can go terribly wrong. When the reality the person with the illness lives in is so skewed, the behaviors that can manifest can be dangerous either to the individual or to others. A realistic look at these co-occurring diseases cannot discount the fact that bad things can and do happen.

Before a diagnosis and the subsequent treatment are found, the symptoms of co-occurring disorders can often be confusing and unpredictable. Hindsight is always 20/20, and many parents have gotten stuck in the quagmire of thinking they could have done something different. In their minds, perhaps disaster could have been averted. Who wouldn't like the gift of knowing that something bad was going to happen before it did so that changes could be made? But those are not the rules we live by, and hard truths must often be learned the hard way.

Take, for instance, the occurrence of school shootings. Of course the parents of any of the shooters would have prevented what happened if they could have. Had they known what was going to take place on the day that their children left the house, they would have stopped it. If they had known a month in advance, a year in advance, they would have put safeguards into place. If only they had known the extent of the illnesses their children suffered from.

Children have yearly physicals at pediatricians' offices, but there is no required yearly mental health well-check visit. And sometimes these diseases, which are hidden from the naked eye, are caught too late. In a forward-thinking and groundbreaking initiative in Massachusetts, the Children's Behavioral Health Initiative was established, which requires all primary care providers to offer standardized behavioral health screenings at well-child visits.[13] Another similar initiative that started in Australia and has begun to take root

---

[13] "Children's Behavioral Health Initiative Overview," Health and Human Services, accessed March 4, 2016, http://www.mass.gov/eohhs/gov/commissions-and-initiatives/cbhi/childrens-behavioral-health-initiative-overview.html.

in America is Young Minds Matter.[14] We can only hope that nationwide, states will recognize the importance of this tool and will require similar initiatives.

As is sometimes the case, reality for a person with co-occurring disorders is the product of a mental illness, meaning that individual's reality does not truly reflect the world around him or her. When an individual is symptomatic, onlookers may easily misread the behaviors they see and may unknowingly make the outcome worse. For instance, this has certainly been true in regards to the law enforcement community in the past. Meeting violent behavior with violent behavior, in this instance, only breeds more of the same. Fortunately, as we have progressed as a society, law enforcement officials are being trained in more effective ways to deal with individuals who are symptomatic because of co-occurring disorders. But as far as we have come, we still have a long way to go.

As funding for mental illnesses and substance use disorders has eroded, the criminal justice system has become our new "state hospital." If circumstances eventually lead to the incarceration of a person with co-occurring disorders, a jail cell can truly be one of the most dangerous places for that person to be. The bottom line is that no matter the situation, a person with co-occurring disorders may not have the skills at different points in life to cope with people who intend to cause him or her harm.

Varying types of trauma to individuals with co-occurring disorders is one likelihood, as they may be seen as an easy target for anything, from having money stolen from them to

---

[14]   Young Minds Matter, accessed March 4, 2016, www.youngmindsmatter.org.au.

being the victims of physical or sexual abuse. In fact, the Adverse Childhood Experience Study (ACES) found that survivors of childhood trauma are up to 5,000 percent more likely to attempt suicide, have eating disorders, or become IV drug users.[15]

Another form of trauma may come from rejection felt from society because of the myths that surround mental illness and addiction. This may come from many different areas, including the church or the criminal justice system. And all of these factors may prove to be too much for the person with the illness to bear. That person may develop a diminished self-image because of the constant feeling of failure originating from society, the family, or his or her own mind.

The mothers that we spoke to talked about dark days and the burden of the knowledge that a lot of men and women don't make it out of these illnesses alive. Whether intended or not, suicide and overdose are a possibility for an individual with co-occurring disorders. In our society, discussing suicide is such a taboo. Individuals who have taken their own lives are often only remembered in hushed terms regarding the events of the suicides rather than for the people they were. Often, anything they may have accomplished in their lives is seemingly erased with them. Suicide is the third leading cause of death in youth aged ten to twenty-four, resulting in about 4,600 deaths per year—that is ten people every day.[16]

---

[15] Robert F. Anda and Vincent J. Felitti, *The ACE Study*.
[16] "Injury Prevention and Control: Division of Violence Prevention," Centers for Disease Control and Prevention, last modified March 10, 2015, http://www.cdc.gov/violenceprevention/suicide/youth_suicide.html.

Where do families go after that? How do they reconcile their faith or other family members to the reality of the diseases that caused their loved ones to take their own lives? The answer is to take their names out of the shadows and remind others that those individuals did not journey in vain. Some have just traveled a road that society as a whole cannot begin to imagine.

When a family experiences something as catastrophic as the death of a loved one, harm inflicted on another person by a loved one, or incarceration of a loved one, it is imperative for the family to find help and not travel this path alone. Whether it's speaking with a professional or crying on the shoulder of a friend, the work of healing can begin. It's difficult to be open about situations like this, but it is very necessary.

In the field of mental illness, addiction, and recovery, it is common to hear strengths-based language, words that are positive rather than negative, from a provider. However, treatment providers who work with people with co-occurring disorders do not have a "Pollyanna" view of these diseases. They are all too aware of how harsh the realities can be. But they also see the other side of the coin. It is one of the jobs of the treatment provider to show families and individuals that there really is hope and recovery.

When a mom experiences the death of her child, regardless of age, there is a hole in her heart that can never be filled. Parents do the best they can for their children and the challenges that they may present. Sadly, sometimes these illnesses are too complex and powerful for the treatments available today.

✧

CHAPTER 6

Recovery Is a Marathon, Not a Sprint

"My husband and I initially blamed ourselves for our child's disease. We thought it was something we could have caused or even prevented with our parenting style. What we learned, though, was not to panic. Things will work out. It just takes longer for some. Once my child started living independently, my outlook improved. It's a slow journey, but we all get there." —A Mother's Perspective

"Fortunately, my husband and I didn't feel too isolated, because we had the continued support of close friends. Al-Anon was also a huge support to me. Honestly, it's hard for me to remember the bad times, even though I know they happened. I am truly enjoying my life now. Perhaps that's the healing gift of time. I think that's the most important thing for other moms to know—time really does heal all wounds." —A Mother's Perspective

One of the best analogies that can be made of the journey to recovery from co-occurring disorders is that of running a marathon. No matter which way you look at it, a marathon is a set distance. Perhaps someone may run it more quickly than others, but at the end of the day, the miles remain the same. Recovery is a journey that requires preparation, training, encouragement, and ongoing support. Long-term care is key for recovery from co-occurring disorders.

It cannot be stated enough that co-occurring disorders are chronic illnesses, and often there are multiple episodes before the progress that an individual has made can be seen. The beauty of recovery is that every single episode or relapse builds on the next. A person living with co-occurring disorders is not back at square one after each episode, even though it may feel like it.

Sometimes a person can be in treatment for a long period of time and then find that it's not going in the right direction. This is especially true if the dual diagnoses are not treated simultaneously. If treatment for the individual with the co-occurring disorders is inadequate for a dual diagnosis, it is imperative that new treatment be found. The experience of changing treatments can be difficult not only for the person with the disease but for the whole family, but sustained recovery is only possible with the right treatment.

Have patience. Finding the right treatment is an investment of time. These are chronic illnesses that don't get better after one twenty-eight-day stay. What may seem like an easy thing to fix for one person may be an entirely different story for another. For some people, maintaining health is achievable after initial hurdles are crossed. For others, especially those with co-occurring illnesses, no amount of will power alone will help the individual overcome the hurdles.

When the individual enters treatment, as much of a relief as it may be for the family, the work is not done. The entire family needs to work at finding new coping skills and supports. It's as much of a marathon for the family as it is for the individual. The same type of preparation that goes into training for a marathon needs to be done when a loved one goes into treatment. Many of the mothers we spoke to said that they needed to prepare themselves for what was ahead as much as their children did.

As one of the moms we talked to put it, "Recovery is not a destination; it's a process." It may take a long time to find effective treatment and for that treatment to yield desired results. When a loved one has co-occurring disorders, the family needs to notice and celebrate small changes, all the while remembering that the individual is most likely much farther along the road to recovery than he or she was even a year prior.

We talk about recovery being a marathon because these are chronic illnesses that by nature occur over time and do not remediate after one treatment. The time a person spends in the throes of a mental illness and substance use disorder is the same amount of time needed for treatment to focus on the change process. The person needs to understand this and decide that it is in his or her best interest to begin recovering. This process requires patience, fortitude, manageable consequences, and the ability to hope for the person who has no hope.

After someone embraces treatment and is sober and stable, the work of recovery can begin. There is no fast track. If someone has joined twelve-step groups, he or she will follow the suggestions of no relationships or major decisions until one year of sobriety. The individual will begin to actively work the steps and will continue the emotional and spiritual transformation for the rest of his or her life. For people who choose other paths of recovery, the process of transformation will still take time and a lot of inner work. Recovery is like an onion, in that people continue to "peel the layers off" as they deepen their recoveries.

Many people experience a relapse during recovery. They may begin to use alcohol or drugs, stop taking medication, or both. This is often the result of increased stress, the surfacing of underlying trauma, or simply becoming successful. Relapses highlight the need for new skills. It is important to understand that relapse occurs only after someone has made a decision and commitment to change.

Often people get labeled as treatment resistant or chronic relapsers, when really they only made the decision to go into treatment to stay out of the hospital or jail, to please their families, or to be allowed to stay in school. When done for these reasons, they have not internalized the need to change for themselves. It is important to ascertain and understand this difference in order to find the best treatment and to help with the frustration, anger, and disappointment that often accompany ongoing mental illness and substance abuse treatment.

Relapses are treatable and often are the gateway to deeper insight, commitment, and recovery. Understanding what precipitated the relapse and learning new coping skills are the focus of treatment. A person does not have to "hit bottom," and treating a relapse can occur immediately.

The healing for families that takes place when they are a part of the treatment process is remarkable. Families are allowed to work through their dark days, just as the person in treatment is working through his or hers. Seeing how long and how much work goes into the act of becoming healthy has been described as humbling by many of the mothers we spoke to. And the progress made by individuals in recovery can be inspiring to their families. Certainly few families could have imagined they would get to the point that recovery, in and of itself, would be inspirational.

Just as the individual in treatment works hard, the family needs to be willing to work equally as hard by investing a significant amount of time in the process. There is no quick fix for the individual or the family. And, as it most likely took the son or daughter a long period of time to become unhealthy, it takes the same kind of time to become healthy once again.

One mother remarked that after treatment, the pieces are not in the same places anymore, but they do fit. A family just needs time to adjust to the changes that have occurred. And as this healing takes place, a family needs to be honest but not to the point that it burdens the son or daughter. Behaviors that manifested due to co-occurring disorders were a symptom of the disease and although perhaps directed at the family, were not the intention of the individual. Self-growth, not blame from a family member, will lead the individual to confront the hard truths of the disease.

In this marathon, the family grows and evolves. The mother of an infant changes as her son or daughter changes and perhaps will grow to parent in a way that she could not have imagined when her child was younger. So too the mother of an individual with co-occurring disorders is no longer the same as she was before the onset of the disease.

People do recover. There is hope. Individuals can learn to live with their illnesses. The individual is not the disease, and his or her identity does not have to be the label that was given to him or her. Everyone has skills and strengths. Mothers need to remember that they are not just mothers of children with an illness. And new growth can occur when they are able to reframe how they look at their children.

⟡

CHAPTER 7

Anchoring Versus Enabling

"My husband and I have been in recovery for a long time. And we have relied on Al-Anon to help us learn to cope with the effects of that disease. We thought that we were prepared, but I suffered a lot until I came to terms with my own child's addiction. I know that other mothers have felt isolated in their journeys, but this wasn't my experience. I learned to feel empowered and was able to be a resource for my child and my family. I meditate, I read about these diseases, and, finally, I turn my fear for my child's life over to God." —A Mother's Perspective

The role of the mother who finds herself parenting an adult child with co-occurring disorders is often filled with uncertainty. How much is too much intervention? How little is too little? And what is true for the role of a parent in general is true for the mother of a son or daughter with COD: there is no manual.

When a parent first brings a child home, there can seem to be an endless amount of advice. "Don't you dare put that baby on his stomach to sleep!" or "Go ahead and put the baby on her belly to sleep. Your grandmother did that with me and I did that with you…we survived!" Bottle versus breast. Cloth versus plastic diaper. What is the right temperature for a bath? How warm should the house be kept? Whether the advice is welcome or not, a new parent doesn't have to look hard to find it. In fact, this holds true even as a child matures and grows into adulthood. It seems that everyone has an opinion and isn't afraid to offer it. Until, that is, an individual starts exhibiting signs of co-occurring disorders.

At first, well-meaning friends or relatives may offer advice that addresses the behaviors they see. "You need to provide more structure; that's what she's missing," or "Lay down the law; you tell him that until he gets his act together, he can't come home." What they may not realize is that the advice they are offering is for an acute condition. When the chronic nature of these diseases manifest, many people may look at the adult child as a lost cause. Advice then gives way to gossip, or perhaps the talking just stops altogether, isolating the family of a loved one with COD even further.

So, the mother of an adult child with co-occurring disorders is left on her own, after so many years of having a seemingly endless amount of advice offered to her. And because she loves her child and wants to protect him or her, she does the best she can. Truly, on this journey, no one can judge what this mother does when she feels she must just keep her son or daughter alive.

An often-used term in regards to parenting an adult child with chronic brain diseases is the word "enabling." Used in a positive nature, this word can refer to empowering another individual to reach goals and find success. Sadly, many mothers of individuals with COD are subjected to the label in a negative connotation. Over the years, enabling has been used to describe behaviors that a loved one does that allow a disease to progress or that cause the disease itself. These behaviors might include giving an individual money that is then used to buy drugs, bailing an individual out of jail, or fixing a speeding or DUI ticket, among other things. These behaviors, which are well meaning at the time, have lasting negative consequences for the individual as well as the family because they continue to support the disease process rather than treatment and recovery.

In reality, most parents are making decisions out of fear without the best information or skills to do anything else. Their goal is to help, which is why family treatment is so important. "Enabling" used in a derogatory manner creates shame, blame, and guilt; the label does nothing to encourage people to learn and change their behaviors. Families are part of the solution when given the tools needed to help themselves and their loved ones.

In regards to the mothers with whom we spoke, we would like to reframe this powerful word. It is true that it can be a behavior that a family does, not knowing better, in order to keep a loved one alive. But, in a way that shames, mothers are all too often told that they enable their children's addictions or symptomatic behaviors. In a mother's mind, though, the act of keeping her child alive is the goal. Historically, the level of impairment is such that without intervention, death is the outcome. What looks to others like enabling can really be the mother anchoring her son or daughter.

Being an anchor means that the mother is there for her adult child. Sometimes she's the care manager, sometimes the crisis intervener. When an individual is incapacitated due to these brain diseases, the need to step in is great. People can still drift, but when a parent is an anchor, they don't drift so far that they get lost in the sea of homelessness, victimization, and addiction.

A mother acting as an anchor keeps her son or daughter connected to the community. She provides a safe place for the person living with co-occurring disorders so that he or she can learn new and effective ways to cope. In this role, she is able to provide consequences that are effective but not punitive. The seeming ambiguity here is that there always needs to be a consequence for a destructive behavior. Of utmost importance, though, is that the consequence meets the behavior.

If the mother's parenting style tended to be lenient before the paranoia, intoxication, or any number of other symptoms set in, and she suddenly puts her foot down, it is not unusual to be met with resistance. If a person isn't used to having limits set, he or she often won't respond when the limit is put into place.

Perhaps the parents didn't intervene sooner because they just could not believe that this was happening to their son or daughter. No matter the reason limits were not in place, it is the psychosis itself that creates resistance, and it is not willful. And if a situation escalates and an individual threatens self-harm, natural instinct prevails, and parents do what they have to in order to keep their child alive.

For single moms, this is an even tougher dynamic. Everything may fall on the shoulders of the mother, including the search for effective treatment and how to pay for a program when it's found. Seeing firsthand the devastating effects of these diseases on her son or daughter, the single mother is not only the first responder but oftentimes the only responder. And she may also bear the heavy burden of being the sole person at whom all of her child's anger is directed. She is often isolated and has no one to share her fears, doubts, and insecurities with—at least, no one who is as invested in her son or daughter as she is.

For all of these reasons, it is imperative for parents to reach out to learn how to cope. When they reach out, they ensure that they and their loved ones will have a safety net in the community. When a safety net is in place and a person with co-occurring disorders falls, he or she doesn't have to fall so hard that life is affected for years to come.

The nature of any chronic illness is such that symptoms can reoccur. The experience for a mother whose child has succeeded in treatment and then has an episode of illness and needs intervention again can feel like another hill on the roller coaster. Taking a step back, though, a family needs to see that every perceived failure is a step closer to recovery and wellness. With other chronic diseases, such as diabetes, for instance, any amount of treatment, as well as reappearing symptoms, is acceptable and even expected. Why is it not the same when it comes to chronic brain diseases?

Co-occurring disorders are diseases that affect the whole family. If a treatment program won't allow families to see their loved ones for the duration of the treatment, the anchors that the individuals will need to rely on when they complete treatment and return to "life as normal" are excluded. We all need anchors in our lives. And this is one of the most natural roles a mother will play. It was undoubtedly the one for which she was intended.

How do people obtain remission from dual disorders?[17]
• stable housing • sober support network / family • regular meaningful activity • trusting clinical relationships

When an individual with co-occurring disorders completes the course of treatment, his or her transition back into the community can be a terrifying time for family members. Fear of what might happen when a child goes back into the community is a very common emotion for parents to feel. When a person with COD is in a residential facility, it may be

---

[17] Alverson et al, Com MNJ, 2000

the first time in a long time that his or her family has collectively been able to take a deep breath. Perhaps, for a moment, they are not consumed by the worry that may have been keeping them up for so many sleepless nights.

In residential treatment, for the participant, time moves at its own pace, which allows the individual the opportunity to heal and learn to become healthy. If a facility is outcomes based, supports are put into place when the individual is ready to transition to independent living. Even with these supports, though, these chronic diseases are in no way gone, and a family has good reason to be concerned. So the fears that a mother experienced before her child went into treatment are revisited. She worries that her child will isolate himself or herself again and wonders if the supports that are in place will be adequate. She worries that the strides her child gained will be lost. And she has no guarantees that she won't find herself back on the same roller coaster.

When an individual is in a residential facility, he or she is closely monitored, and issues that may arise can be handled on the spot. For instance, if a medication does not seem to be effective, a nurse or physician on staff can make an adjustment as soon as the team is made aware of the fact. And while the medication may not have been as effective as necessary, the individual was in the safe confines of treatment. When an individual transitions out of a residential situation, the efficacy of the medication he or she receives is of paramount concern. Adding to the struggle of finding the right medication is the fact that because of the side effects of some medications, people stop taking them.

Amid these concerns, the mother may have a hard time simply knowing her role again. She may find herself relearning how she fits in the life of her son or daughter. She was the first responder for so long that it may be difficult to give up this role. Of the mothers we interviewed, one of the common themes was that they had a hard time letting go. As much as a mother wants to be an anchor for her child, she begins to realize that her child needs to experience life and make his or her own choices.

There is a great paradox in parenting. Parents may grieve the loss of their sweet, innocent child as he or she matures. But they know that a child maturing and growing away from them is a natural part of the process. For the parents of an individual with COD, this is just as true. The growing up and growing away sometimes just happens later in their child's life than in the life of someone without COD.

"In order to realize the worth of the anchor, we need to feel the stress of the storm." Corrie ten Boom

CHAPTER 8

Reclaiming Your Life

"I have learned to reach out to others for help. It really is amazing how many people are having the same experience as you, and you may not even have realized it. I prayed a lot and journaled, and my small community was a huge help. I would tell other mothers to be patient and don't give up. Co-occurring disorders are a journey, and change will not happen overnight." —A Mother's Perspective

"In the beginning, I felt so isolated and alone. But finding a support system and even being able to help teach others has been huge for me. My family, my church, and the special group of ladies in the Bible study I attend have seen me through this otherwise lonely journey." —A Mother's Perspective

Once the extreme highs and lows of illness, diagnosis, treatment, and recovery begin to stabilize, the mother needs to work on finding where and how all of the pieces fit—how she herself fits, not only in the life of her son or daughter but also in society in general. The landscape of her family may have changed significantly since the onset of the co-occurring disorder. There might have been marriages, divorces, remarriages, deaths, and even births of new family members. The world around the family likely changed greatly since last they lifted their heads to look around.

A mother may have put her dreams on hold for a very long time, only to find that those dreams are not relevant to her anymore. Or perhaps they are. Either way, this is the time that she needs to look ahead and think of her own needs. The amount of time that goes into helping a family member with co-occurring disorders takes an emotional toll. As an individual continues to improve and get well, the role that a parent plays will change and mature.

Not only does she need to think of her own needs, but she also needs to focus on letting go. Old fears may return. While most people do well while in treatment, transitioning out of that treatment can be terrifying to parents: She's out with the car, is she safe? Will he become the victim of bullying once again? Will she relapse or stop taking her medication? Waiting for the other shoe to drop is exhausting in and of itself. A mother may have to learn how to handle her adult child's success and independence just as she learned how to navigate the failures and necessary dependence.

When there are matters of life and death, thinking of anything other than what is going on in the here and now proves to be very difficult. A woman may find that she doesn't even know what she likes anymore. Having focused her energy and life on finding effective treatment and keeping her son or daughter alive, she is left with little time for self-reflection. When a woman has been without things in life that support her well-being for a sustained period of time, perhaps she will find it hard to even say what these things may be. As the individual with co-occurring disorders improves, the void in the life of the parent becomes more noticeable, because so much time and energy was expended in the process of recovery. The mother's grief may have given way to depression, and she will need to seek treatment for herself. She may have stopped exercising or cooking, and her relationships with friends and family may have wilted. This is indeed the time for her to focus on her own life.

Because of the toll that chronic illnesses take, many developmental milestones will not be reached in the same timeframe as that of a person without a chronic illness. Sons and daughters may not have moved away after graduation from high school, or they quickly came back home. The individual may have never had a romantic relationship. An individual who may not have been able to function independently for years may seem to be suddenly on his or her own. The process of letting go while an individual becomes more independent is hard under even the healthiest of circumstances.

It is common in early recovery for adults with COD to go through adolescent development, regardless of the age that they are when they become sober. It may be surprising to parents that they need to face these issues again. Emotional development stops at the onset of substance use or mental illness, and so part of the experience in recovery as a parent is that the adult child goes through this phase once they become healthy. Al-Anon and NAMI can be a huge help when navigating these waters.

Learning how, when, and where to let go is key for the parent of an individual with co-occurring disorders. There is a significant need for support for the growth of an individual who is learning to become independent after lengthy illnesses. Unfortunately, there is no manual or safety net, and this process can be purely trial and error. And trial and error, as a parent lets go while the individual gains autonomy, is how that person will learn.

There are a number of different areas through which a mother can find support: NAMI, Family-to-Family groups, Al-Anon, or a local church, just to name a few. Families really need as much support as their loved ones who are active in treatment and recovery from co-occurring disorders. After treatment, a comprehensive discharge plan is imperative for the whole family. The plan needs to clearly outline the community supports involved. Having this plan will take some of the burden off of the shoulders of the mother.

Recovery creates its own set of stressors and new skills to be developed. A comprehensive discharge plan may highlight the need to make changes within a family. A family may need to take a look at its own substance use issues. Reintegrating a family member into the larger family when other members have fear and misconceptions is also a huge hurdle to cross. Coming to terms with who the individual has become, as opposed to who the parent and family as a whole may have hoped he or she would be, can be easier said than done.

It may not come as a surprise that the journey for siblings of the person with co-occurring disorders can parallel what the parent goes though. The siblings may have moved on or away or have their own issues because of what they experienced during the course of these illnesses. Because of this, those siblings may not be the best people to fill in when the parents are gone. Parents and siblings need to determine the level of involvement and the kind of support the siblings can be for their loved one. It is imperative for the siblings to seek their own supports and treatments to resolve issues and gain forgiveness.

And while there is certainly respite while in treatment, outside of the safe confines of treatment, feelings of desperation and fear can be created by the lack of community-based resources. For a parent, it can be frightening when the son or daughter begins to form new social relationships with people who aren't in or from the recovery world.

As a whole, we are interdependent beings. Good communication skills and supports help us all to avoid the pitfalls of codependence. Interdependence is defined as the mutual dependence between individuals. It is different from codependence, which is more harmful than helpful. With individuals who need extra supports to be successful, the focus needs to be on interdependence and recovery. Interdependence should be celebrated. When an individual takes one step forward and then takes another step back, it doesn't have to be a catastrophe, but instead can be a learning experience. Anyone who is learning to ride a bike can fall off the first time, but given the right support and time, they'll figure it out.

And so this is when a mother can begin to detach and focus on her own life. Can I travel? Can I go back to school? Can I become involved in a civic organization? This is where she learns who she is, and it is her time for herself. She is likely very different than she was before her child went into treatment. Before these illnesses shaped her. And, finally, she may now have hope where she didn't before as she comes to terms with the fact that there are new dreams.

The mothers that we spoke to say it's imperative to create new boundaries. It's also important to find people to bond with who understand the experience. For many of the mothers, it has been good to write things down in a journal. Writing not about her son or daughter but rather about herself. It becomes a place where she can express how she felt then and how she feels now. And as ardently as a mother may have searched for treatment for her loved one, she now needs to search for healing for herself.

The journey has been long and exhausting, but what was accomplished makes way for new growth, new dreams, and new opportunities. On one hand, the journey could be compared to the destructive force of a wildfire. But, when an individual takes a step back to look at the bigger picture, they can see that the other attribute of fire is one of cleansing. What is old can be removed to make way for something new and more beautiful than the family may ever have imagined. Hope and healing are often the products of integrated treatment for co-occurring disorders.

APPENDIX A:

◦✖◦

Questions for Families to Ask When Looking for a Treatment Program

1. Does the treatment program include families?

   a. If so, describe the treatment and the outcome.

2. Does the program treat people with co-occurring disorders?

   a. If so, define the illnesses that are treated (i.e., schizophrenia, depression, PTSD, borderline personality disorder, etc.) It is vital that you confirm that the treatment program is able to treat the illness that your family member experiences.

3. Does the program provide integrated treatment for dual disorders?

   a. If so, ensure that it takes into account all seven components of integrated treatment; Integration,

Comprehensiveness, Assertiveness, Reduction of negative consequences, Long-term perspective, Motivation-based treatment, Multiple psychotherapeutic modalities.

4. What are the outcomes for the program?

    a. What do they measure?

    b. For how long do they measure?

5. Can I speak to alumni, either an individual or a family?

6. Is this program in network for insurance?

    a. If so, which ones?

    b. If out of network for insurance, what is the program's billing practice?

    c. Has the program been successful in helping families access their benefits?

7. Will the family have access to the treatment team?

8. What is the program's policy around medication?

9. What is the program's policy around opiate replacement therapy?

Stages of Change for Families

Stage	Presentation	Treatment	Family Focus	What to Expect
Pre-contemplation	Person believes the "problem" is a result of external issues such as work, school, parents, etc. Sees the problem as a solution. May feel hopeless.	Focus is on relationship building, assessments, education, and developing ambivalence. Consciousness raising. Targeting thoughts.	Focus on behavior. Non-judgmental approach. Seek integrated treatment of mental illness and substance abuse. Get help for yourself. NAMI Family-to-Family, Al-Anon, other support groups, counseling.	The goal is to develop insight into the "problem." Look for thoughts that reflect ambivalence. Behavior will not change.

Stage	Presentation	Treatment	Family Focus	What to Expect
Contemplation	May talk about changing. May begin to talk about having a problem. Ambivalence is very apparent.	Change perception, to internalize "what's in it for me" if they change. Resolve ambivalence. Targeting perceptions.	Ask about the benefits of substance use and symptoms of mental illness. Talk about healthy decision making; help to resolve ambivalence. Continue self-care.	May talk about the "problem" and wanting to change. May be talking the talk, however behavior does not change. Frustration may occur due to this dialectic. The decision to change may happen as a result of a consequence or illness; it is a process. Behavior does not change.

Stage	Presentation	Treatment	Family Focus	What to Expect
Preparation	Engaged in treatment. Talking about changing, beginning to try recovery solutions, hopeful. Has made a commitment to change.	Shift in behaviors. Practice using new skills. Increase self-confidence and self-esteem. Develop a sober and healthy support system. Target behavior.	Anxiety around the adaptation of new skills and fear of failure. Be supportive. Work on self-care.	Recovery behaviors are evident. Perceptions of the problem have changed and thoughts have changed.
Action	Changing behavior to recovery behaviors. Hopeful, moving on with life.	Use rewards to reinforce new behavior. Work on managing symptoms of mental illness and practicing sober skills. Target behavior, thoughts, and perceptions.	Support sober lifestyle. Reward achievements. Develop a plan for relapse/lapse. **Remember: Recovery is one day at a time**. Continue self-care.	Requesting more independence and autonomy. Looking to find a new place and identity in the family. Renewing hobbies and activities. Healthy lifestyle changes.

Stage	Presentation	Treatment	Family Focus	What to Expect
Maintenance	Maintaining new behaviors. Hopeful, engaged in the community and family.	Learn new skills as life unfolds. May begin more in-depth therapy. Target behavior, thoughts, and perceptions.	Support sober lifestyle. Reward achievements, develop a plan for relapse/lapse. **Remember: Recovery is one day at a time**. Continue self-care. Episodes of illness are common…be prepared. Familiarize yourself with your loved one's Crisis Plan.	Increased self-confidence. Has a role in the community. Active in recovery groups and tasks. Healthy lifestyle changes.

Resources

Suggested Reading List

- Alcoholics Anonymous. *Alcoholics Anonymous.* New York: Alcoholics Anonymous World Services, Inc., 2001.

- Alcoholics Anonymous. *Twelve Steps and Twelve Traditions.* New York: Alcoholics Anonymous World Services, Inc., 2002.

- Amador, Xavier, and Anna-Lisa Johanson. *I Am Not Sick I Don't Need Help: Helping the Seriously Mentally Ill Accept Treatment.* New York: Vida Press, 2000.

- Cardwell, Dave, *No More Secrets: A Courageous Journey through Tragedy to Recovery,* Rock Hill, SC: Overcomer Press, 2002.

– Chamberlin, Judi. *On Our Own: Patient-Controlled Alternatives to the Mental Health System*. Lawrence, MA: National Empowerment Center, 1977.

– Copeland, Mary Ellen, *The Depression Workbook: A Guide for Living with Depression and Manic Depression*. Oakland, CA: New Harbinger Publications, 2001.

– Dickens, Rex, and Diane Marsh, eds. *Anguished Voices: Siblings and Adult Children of Persons with Psychiatric Disabilities*. Boston: Boston University, Center for Psychiatric Rehabilitation, 1994.

– Fawcett, Jan, Bernard Golden, and Nancy Rosenfeld. *New Hope for People with Bipolar Disorder: Your Friendly, Authoritative Guide to the Latest in Traditional and Complementary Solutions*. Roseville, CA: Prima Publishing, 2000.

– Fletcher, Anne. *Sober for Good: New Solutions for Drinking Problems—Advice from Those Who Have Succeeded*. New York: Houghton Mifflin Company, 2001.

– Gottesman, Irving. *Schizophrenia Genesis: The Origins of Madness*. New York: Henry Holt and Company, 1990.

– Jamison, Kay. *An Unquiet Mind: A Memoir of Moods and Madness*. New York: Vintage Books, 1995.

– Keefe, Richard, and Philip Harvey. *Understanding Schizophrenia: A Guide to the New Research on Causes and Treatment*. New York: Free Press, 1994.

- Marsh, Diane, and Rex Dickens. *How to Cope with Mental Illness in Your Family: A Self-Care Guide for Siblings, Offspring, and Parents.* New York: Jeremy P. Tarcher, 1997.

- McCollom, Eric, and Terry Trepper. *Family Solutions for Substance Abuse: Clinical and Counseling Approaches.* New York: The Haworth Clinical Practice Press, 2001.

- Mueser, Kim, and Susan Gingerich. *Coping With Schizophrenia: A Guide for Families,* New Oakland, CA: Harbinger Publications, 1994.

- Prochaska, James, John Norcross, and Carlo Diclemente. *Changing for Good: A Revolutionary Six-Stage Program for Overcoming Bad Habits and Moving Your Life Positively Forward,* New York: HarperCollins, 1994.

- Rapp, Charles. *The Strengths Model: A Recovery-Oriented Approach to Mental Health Services.* New York: Oxford University Press, 1998.

- Ruden, Ronald, and Marcia Byalick. *The Craving Brain: A Bold New Approach to Breaking Free from Drug Addiction, Overeating, Alcoholism, and Gambling.* New York: HarperCollins, 2000.

- Stimmel, Barry. *Alcoholism, Drug Addiction, and the Road to Recovery: Life on the Edge.* New York: The Haworth Medical Press, 2002.

- Temes, Roberta. *Getting Your Life Back Together When You Have Schizophrenia.* Oakland, CA: New Harbinger Publications, 2002.

– Torrey, E. Fuller. *Surviving Schizophrenia: A Manual for Families, Consumers, and Providers.* New York: HarperCollins, 1995.

– Vonnegut, Mark. *The Eden Express: A Memoir of Insanity.* New York: Seven Stories Press, 1975.

– Woods, Mary Ryan, and Katherine Armstrong. *When the Door Opened:* Stories of Recovery from Co-occurring Mental Illness & Substance Use Disorders. Manchester, NH: WestBridge, 2012.

– Woolis, Rebecca. *When Someone You Love Has a Mental Illness: A Handbook for Families and Friends.* New York: Jeremy P. Tarcher, 1992.

Blogs

Addiction Blog: An online community of writers exploring best practices in addiction treatment. http://www.addictionblog.org

WestBridge Blog: A blog that discusses dual diagnoses issues. http://www.westbridge.org/news-resources/blog

Magazines

Bp Magazine. http://www.bphope.com
SZ Magazine. http://mentalwellnesstoday.com/sz-magazine/

Online Resources

American Mental Health Alliance: This organization developed out of the Coalition of Mental Health Professionals & Consumers as an alternative mental health delivery system and advocacy. They are not-for-profit and fight for client privacy, confidentiality, and freedom of choice.[18]

http://www.americanmentalhealth.com

Bazelon Center for Mental Health Law: The mission of the Judge David L. Bazelon Center for Mental Health Law is to protect and advance the rights of adults and children who have mental disabilities. The Bazelon Center envisions an America where people who have mental illnesses or developmental disabilities exercise their own life choices and have access to the resources that enable them to participate fully in their communities.[19]

http://www.bazelon.org

Depression and Bipolar Support Alliance: Provides information and advocacy on depression and bipolar issues. This group was previously known as the Depression and Bipolar Support Association and also as the National Depressive and Manic-Depressive Association.[20]

http://www.dbsalliance.org

---

[18] "Advocacy and Policy: Resources," PsychCentral, accessed March 4, 2016, http://psychcentral.com/resources/Mental_Health/Advocacy_and_Policy/.

[19] "Who We Are," Judge David L. Bazelon Center for Mental Health Law, accessed March 4, 2016, http://www.bazelon.org/Who-We-Are.aspx.

[20] "Advocacy and Policy: Resources."

Dual Recovery Anonymous: Dual Recovery Anonymous is an independent, nonprofessional, Twelve Step, mutual support membership organization for people with a dual diagnosis. Our goal is to help men and women who experience a dual illness. We are chemically dependent and we are also affected by an emotional or psychiatric illness.[21] http://www.draonline.org

Mental Health America: Formerly known as the National Mental Health Association. Mental Health America's Advocacy Network is a powerful voice for change that is made up of thousands of individuals nationwide who take an active role in protecting America's mental health.[22] http://www.mentalhealthamerica.net

Mental Health Legal Advisors Committee: Provides legal assistance to mental health consumers. Offers variety of publications related to patient's rights.[23] http://www.mhlac.org

M-POWER's Mental Health Advocacy: M-POWER is the Massachusetts statewide mental health advocacy organization. http://www.m-power.org

NAMI (National Alliance on Mental Illness): The nation's largest grassroots mental health organization

---

[21] "Welcome to the DRA Online Resource Center."
[22] "Advocacy and Policy: Resources."
[23] "Advocacy and Policy: Resources."

dedicated to building better lives for the millions of Americans affected by mental illness. What started as a small group of families gathered around a kitchen table in 1979 has blossomed into the nation's leading voice on mental health. Today, we are an association of hundreds of local affiliates, state organizations and volunteers who work in your community to raise awareness and provide support and education that was not previously available to those in need. NAMI relies on gifts and contributions to support our important work.[24] http://www.nami.org

The National Association for the Dually Diagnosed: NADD is a not-for-profit membership association established for professionals, care providers and families to promote understanding of and services for individuals who have developmental disabilities and mental health needs.[25] http://thenadd.org

The National Council: The National Council for Community Behavioral Healthcare is a not-for-profit 501(c)(3) association representing 1,300 organizations providing treatment and rehabilitation to help people recover from mental illnesses and addiction disorders.[26] http://www.thenationalcouncil.org

---

[24] "About NAMI," National Alliance on Mental Illness, accessed March 3, 2016, https://www.nami.org/About-NAMI.

[25] "About Us," NADD, accessed March 4, 2016, http://thenadd.org/about-nadd/.

[26] "Advocacy and Policy: Resources."

National Institute of Mental Health: The National Institute of Mental Health (NIMH) is the lead federal agency for research on mental disorders. NIMH is one of the 27 Institutes and Centers that make up the National Institutes of Health (NIH), the nation's medical research agency. NIH is part of the U.S. Department of Health and Human Services (HHS).[27]

http://www.nimh.nih.gov/index.shtml

National Suicide Prevention Lifeline: The National Suicide Prevention Lifeline provides free and confidential emotional support to people in suicidal crisis or emotional distress 24 hours a day, 7 days a week. Since its inception, the Lifeline has engaged in a variety of initiatives to improve crisis services and advance suicide prevention.[28]

www.suicidepreventionlifeline.org

Office of the Healthcare Advocate: OHA is dedicated to serving and assisting Connecticut's healthcare consumers in understanding and exercising their appeal rights for denial of benefit or service under their healthcare plan. Check with your state to see if they have an equivalent program.

www.ct.gov/oha

Substance Abuse and Mental Health Services Administration: The Substance Abuse and Mental Health

---

[27]   "About NIMH," National Institute of Mental Health, accessed March 4, 2016, http://www.nimh.nih.gov/about/index.shtml.

[28]   "Lifeline Overview," National Suicide Prevention Lifeline, accessed March 4, 2016, http://www.suicidepreventionlifeline.org/about/overview.aspx.

Services Administration (SAMHSA) is the agency within the U.S. Department of Health and Human Services that leads public health efforts to advance the behavioral health of the nation. SAMHSA's mission is to reduce the impact of substance abuse and mental illness on America's communities.[29] http://www.samhsa.gov

The Treatment Advocacy Center: The Treatment Advocacy Center is a national 501(c)3 nonprofit organization dedicated to eliminating legal and other barriers to the timely and effective treatment of severe mental illness. The organization promotes laws, policies and practices for the delivery of psychiatric care and supports the development of innovative treatments for and research into the causes of severe and persistent psychiatric illnesses, such as schizophrenia and bipolar disorder.[30]
http://www.treatmentadvocacycenter.org

VoiceAmerica

One Hour AT A Time with Mary Woods is a recovery and wellness-oriented Internet radio broadcast hosted by WestBridge's Mary Woods and Jonathan Routhier, which brings in tens of thousands of listeners per month. Not only can you listen to the shows live through a streaming feature on the web, you can also download any past episodes to listen

---

[29] "Who We Are," Substance Abuse and Mental Health Services Administration, last modified December 18, 2015, http://www.samhsa.gov/about-us/who-we-are.
[30] "A Short History," The Treatment Advocacy Center, accessed March 4, 2016, http://www.treatmentadvocacycenter.org/about-us/our-history.

to at your convenience. The show attracts guests from a variety of disciplines in the addiction and mental health realms who share their compassion and knowledge with listeners. According to the VoiceAmerica Network, "*One Hour AT A Time* has proven to be an educational and high-quality program since the show launch in October of 2007…[and] has reliably ranked in the top three VoiceAmerica Health and Wellness programs for listeners."

One Hour AT A Time airs on the VoiceAmerica Health and Wellness Channel every Monday afternoon at 3:00 P.M. EST. To tune in or browse older episodes to download, visit the WestBridge website for more information.

ᐦᕦᐦ

Frequently Used Acronyms

ACT—assertive community treatment

ADL—activities of daily living

AIMS—Abnormal Involuntary Movement Scale

BAC—blood alcohol content (or blood alcohol concentration)

BDI—Beck Depression Inventory

CBT—cognitive-behavioral therapy

CIWA—Clinical Institute Withdrawal Assessment of Alcohol

DAU—drugs of abuse in urine

DBT—dialectical behavior therapy

EBP—evidence-based practice

EMR—electronic medical record

FES—family education and support

HIPAA—Health Insurance Portability and Accountability Act

ICS—integrated clinical summary

IDDT—integrated dual disorder treatment

IMR—illness management and recovery

IOP—intensive outpatient program

LOS—length of stay

PAA—personal achievement agenda

PAG—personal achievement goal

PTSD—post-traumatic stress disorder

SNAP—strengths, needs, abilities, and preferences

SPMI—severe and persistent mental illness

TBI—traumatic brain injury

VASA—Violence and Suicide Assessment

WB—WestBridge

WRAP—Wellness Recovery Action Plan

Mental Health Organizations/Titles

AAAP—American Academy of Addiction Psychiatry

AMHCA—American Mental Health Counselors Association

APA—American Psychiatric Association

APNA—American Psychiatric Nurses Association

ARNP—Advanced Registered Nurse Practitioner

ARTA—American Residential Treatment Association

ASAM—American Society of Addiction Medicine

CADAC—Certified Alcohol and Drug Addiction Counselor

CARF—Commission on Accreditation of Rehabilitation Facilities

CSAT—Center for Substance Abuse Treatment

CSAP—Center for Substance Abuse Prevention

DSM—Diagnostic and Statistical Manual of Mental Disorders

MOAR—Massachusetts Organization for Addiction Recovery

NAADAC—National Association for Alcoholism and Drug Abuse Counselors

NAATP—National Association of Addiction Treatment Providers

NAMI—National Alliance on Mental Illness

NASW—National Association of Social Workers

NIMH—National Institute of Mental Health

NPI—National Provider Identifier (this is an ID number assigned)

SAMHSA—Substance Abuse and Mental Health Services Administration

ᘛᘚ

Glossary of Technical Terms

This glossary is of technical terms that are associated with several mental health disorders. For example, bulimia is not in this glossary because it is rarely encountered except among eating disorders, and the reader wishing to learn about this symptom should refer to the texts on those disorders. On the other hand, such symptoms as delusions, phobias, obsessions, and depersonalizations are included because they all occur in a number of mental disorders. Many of the entries list the disorders in which the symptom most frequently occurs; it should be understood, however, that the symptom may also be present in other disorders.

advocate. (1) One that pleads the cause of another. Specifically, one that pleads the cause of another before a tribunal or judicial court. (2) One that defends or maintains a cause or proposal. (3) One that supports or promotes the interests of another.[31]

affect. A pattern of observable behaviors that is the expression of a subjectively experienced feeling state (emotion). Common examples of affect are euphoria, anger, and sadness. Affect is variable over time, in response to changing emotional states, whereas mood refers to a pervasive and sustained emotion.

A range of affect may be described as *broad* (normal), *restricted* (constricted), *blunted,* or *flat.* What is considered the normal range of the expression of affect varies considerably, both within and among different cultures. The normal expression of affect involves variability in facial expression, pitch of voice, and hand and body movements. Restricted affect is characterized by a clear reduction in the expressive range and intensity of affects. Blunted affect is marked by a severe reduction in the intensity of affective expression. In flat affect there is virtually no affective expression; generally the voice is monotonous and the face immobile.

Affect is *inappropriate* when it is clearly discordant with the content of the person's speech or ideation. Example: A patient smiled and laughed while discussing demons that were persecuting him.

Affect is *labile* when it is characterized by repeated, rapid, and abrupt shifts. Examples: An elderly man is tearful one moment and combative the next; a young woman is observed by her friends to be friendly,

---

[31] "Advocate," Merriam-Webster.com, accessed March 3, 2016, http://www.merriam-webster.com/dictionary/advocate.

gregarious, and happy one moment and angry and abusive the next, without apparent reason.

agitation. *See* psychomotor agitation.

Al-Anon. Al-Anon is a mutual support group and worldwide fellowship that offers a program of recovery for the families and friends of alcoholics, whether or not the alcoholic recognizes the existence of a drinking problem or seeks help. See more at www.al-anon.org.

anchor. A person or thing that can be relied on for support, stability, or security; mainstay.[32]

anxiety. Apprehension, tension, or uneasiness that stems from the anticipation of danger, which may be internal or external. Some definitions of anxiety distinguish it from fear by limiting it to anticipation of a danger whose source is largely unknown, whereas fear is the response to a consciously recognized and usually external threat of danger. The manifestations of anxiety and fear are the same and include motor tension, autonomic hyperactivity, apprehensive expectation, and vigilance and scanning.

Anxiety may be focused on an object, situation, or activity, which is avoided (phobia), or may be unfocused (free-floating anxiety). It may be experienced in discrete periods of sudden onset and be accompanied by physical symptoms (panic attacks). When anxiety is focused on physical signs or symptoms and causes preoccupation with the fear of belief of having a disease, it is termed hypochondria.

attention. The ability to focus in a sustained manner on one

---

[32] "Anchor," Dictionary.com, accessed March 3, 2016, http://dictionary.reference.com/browse/anchor.

activity. A disturbance in attention may be manifested by difficulty in finishing tasks that have been started, easy distractibility, or difficulty in concentrating on work.

bipolar disorder. Bipolar disorder, formerly called manic depression, causes extreme mood swings that include emotional highs (mania or hypomania) and lows (depression). When you become depressed, you may feel sad or hopeless and lose interest or pleasure in most activities. When your mood shifts in the other direction, you may feel euphoric and full of energy. Mood shifts may occur only a few times a year or as often as several times a week. Although bipolar disorder is a disruptive, long-term condition, you can keep your moods in check by following a treatment plan. In most cases, bipolar disorder can be controlled with medications and psychological counseling (psychotherapy).[33]

blocking. Interruption of a train of speech before a thought or idea has been completed. After a period of silence, which may last from a few seconds to minutes, the person indicates that he or she cannot recall what he or she has been saying or meant to say. Blocking should be judged to be present only if the person spontaneously describes losing his or her train of thought or if, upon questioning by an interviewer, gives that as the reason for pausing.

catatonic behavior. Marked motor anomalies, generally limited to disturbances within the context of a diagnosis of nonorganic psychotic disorder.

---

[33] "Diseases and Conditions: Bipolar Disorder," Mayo Clinic, last modified February 10, 2015, http://www.mayoclinic.org/diseases-conditions/bipolar-disorder/basics/definition/con-20027544.

catatonic excitement. Excited motor activity, apparently purposeless and not influenced by external stimuli.

catatonic negativism. An apparently motiveless resistance to all instructions or attempts to be moved. When passive, the person may resist any effort to be moved; when active, he or she may do the opposite of what is asked—for example, firmly clench jaws when asked to open mouth.

catatonic posturing. Voluntary assumption of an inappropriate or bizarre posture, usually held for a long period of time. Example: A patient may stand with arms outstretched as if he were Jesus on the cross.

catatonic rigidity. Maintenance of a rigid posture against all efforts to be moved.

catatonic stupor. Marked decrease in reactivity to the environment and reduction in spontaneous movements and activity, sometimes to the point of appearing to be unaware of one's surroundings.

catatonic waxy flexibility. The person's limbs can be "molded" into any position, which is then maintained. When the limb is being moved, it feels to the examiner as if it were made of pliable wax.

Celebrate Recovery. A Christ-centered program with foundations firmly established in Biblical truth. The 12 Steps with accompanying Scriptures and the 8 Principles based on the Beatitudes offer participants a clear path of salvation and discipleship; bringing hope, freedom, sobriety, healing, and the opportunity to give back one day at a time through our one and only true Higher Power, Jesus Christ. The 12 Steps and the 8 Principles work seamlessly together, tying historical recovery to timeless Biblical teaching.[34]

circumstantiality. A term used to describe speech that is indirect and delayed in reaching the point because of unnecessary, tedious details and parenthetical remarks. Circumstantial replies or statements may be prolonged for many minutes if the speaker is not interrupted and urged to get to the point. Interviewers often respond to circumstantiality by interrupting the speaker in order to complete the process of history making within an allotted time. This may make it difficult to distinguish loosening of associations from circumstantiality. In the former there is a lack of connection between clauses, but in the latter the clauses always retain a meaningful connection. In loosening of associations, the original point is lost, where as in circumstantiality, the speaker is always aware of the original point, goal, or topic.

Circumstantiality is common in an obsessive-compulsive personality disorder and in many people without mental disorder.

clanging. Speech in which sounds, rather than meaningful, conceptual relationships, govern word choice; it may include rhyming and punning. The term is generally applied only when it is a manifestation of a pathological condition; thus, it would not be used to describe the rhyming word

---

34 "Celebrate Recovery: About Us: 12 Steps," Celebrate Recovery, accessed March 3, 2016, https://www.celebraterecovery.com/index.php/about-us/twelve-steps.

play of children. Example: "I'm not trying to make noise. I'm trying to make sense. If you can make sense out of nonsense, well, have fun. I'm trying to make sense out of sense. I'm not making sense (cents) anymore. I have to make dollars."

Clanging is observed most commonly in schizophrenia and manic episodes.

compulsion. Repetitive and seemingly purposeful behavior that is in response to an obsession, or performed according to certain rules or in a stereotyped fashion. The behavior is not an end in itself, but is designed to produce or prevent some future state of affairs; the activity, however, either is not connected in a realistic way with the state of affairs it is designed to produce or prevent, or may be clearly excessive. The act is performed with a sense of subjective compulsion coupled with a desire to resist it (as least initially); performing the particular act is not pleasurable, although it may afford some relief of tension. Example: A person feels compelled to wash her hands every time she shakes hands because of a fear of contamination, which she recognizes as excessive.

Compulsions are characteristics of obsessive-compulsive disorder.

confabulation. Fabrication of facts or events in response to questions about situations or events that are not recalled because of memory impairment. It differs from lying in that the person is not consciously attempting to deceive.

Confabulation is common in amnesic disorder and in Koriskoff's syndrome.

defense mechanisms. Patterns of feelings, thoughts, or behaviors that are relatively voluntary and arise in response to perceptions of psychic danger. They are designed to hide or alleviate the conflicts or stressors that give rise to anxiety. Some defense mechanisms, such as projection, splitting, and acting out, are almost invariably maladaptive. Others, such as suppression and denial, may be either maladaptive or adaptive, depending on their severity, their inflexibility, and the context in which they occur. Defense mechanisms that are usually adaptive, such as sublimation and humor, are not included here.

> **acting out.** A mechanism in which the person acts without reflection or apparent regard for negative consequences.

> **denial.** When a person is faced with a fact that is too uncomfortable to accept and rejects it instead, insisting that it is not true despite what may be overwhelming evidence.

> **devaluation.** A mechanism in which the person attributes exaggeratedly negative qualities to self or others.

> **displacement.** A mechanism in which the person generalizes or redirects a feeling about an object or a response to an object onto another, usually less-threatening object.

> **dissociation.** A mechanism in which the person sustains a temporary alteration in the integrative functions of consciousness or identity.

> **idealization.** A mechanism in which the person

attributes exaggeratedly positive qualities to self or others.

intellectualization. A mechanism in which the person engages in excessive abstract thinking to avoid experiencing disturbing feelings.

isolation. A mechanism in which the person devises reassuring or self-serving, but incorrect, explanations for his or her own or others' behavior.

passive aggression. A mechanism in which the person indirectly and unassertively expresses aggression towards others.

projection. A mechanism in which the person falsely attributes his or her own unacknowledged feelings, impulses, or thoughts to others.

rationalization. A mechanism in which the person devises reassuring or self-serving, but incorrect, explanations for his or her own or others' behavior.

reaction formation. A mechanism in which the person substitutes behavior, thoughts, or feelings that are diametrically opposed to his or her own unacceptable ones.

repression. A mechanism in which the person is unable to remember or be cognitively aware of disturbing wishes, feelings, thoughts, or experiences.

somatization. A mechanism in which the person becomes preoccupied with physical symptoms disproportionate to any actual physical disturbance.

splitting. A mechanism in which the person views

himself or herself or others as all good or all bad, failing to integrate the positive and negative qualities of self and others into cohesive images; often the person alternately idealizes and devalues the same person.

suppression. A mechanism in which the person intentionally avoids thinking about disturbing problems, desires, feelings, or experiences.

undoing. A mechanism in which the person engages in behavior designed to symbolically make amends for or negate previous thoughts, feelings, or actions.

delusion. A false personal belief based on incorrect inferences about external reality and firmly sustained in spite of what almost everyone else believes and in spite of what constitutes incontrovertible and obvious proof or evidence to the contrary. The belief is not one ordinarily accepted by other members of the person's culture or subculture (i.e., it is not an article of religious faith).

When a false belief involves an extreme value judgment, it is regarded as a delusion only when the judgment is so extreme as to defy credibility. Example: If someone claims he or she is terrible and has disappointed his or her family, this is generally not regarded as a delusion, even if an objective assessment of the situation would lead observers to think otherwise; but if someone claims he or she is the worst sinner in the world, this would generally be considered a delusional conviction. Similarly, a person judged by most people to be moderately underweight who asserts that he or she is fat would not be regarded as delusional, but a person with anorexia nervosa who is at the point of extreme emaciation and insists he or she is fat could rightly be considered delusional.

A delusion should be distinguished from a hallucination, which is a false sensory perception (although a hallucination may give rise to the delusion that the perception is true). A delusion is also to be distinguished from an overvalued idea, in which an unreasonable belief or idea is not as firmly held as in the case of delusion.

delusion of being controlled. A delusion in which feelings, impulses, thoughts, or actions are experienced as being not one's own, as being imposed by some external force. This does not include the mere conviction that one is acting as an agent of God, has had a curse placed on him or her, is the victim of fate, or is not sufficiently assertive. The symptom should be judged present only when the subject experiences his or her will, thoughts, or feelings as operating under some external force. Examples: A man claims that his words are not his own, but rather those of his father; a student believes that his actions are under the control of yogi; a housewife believes that sexual feelings are being put into her body from without.

delusion, bizarre. A false belief that involves a phenomenon that the person's culture would regard as totally implausible. Example: A man believes that when his adenoids were removed in childhood, a box and wires had been placed in his head so that the voice he heard was that of the governor.

delusion, grandiose. A delusion whose content involves an exaggerated sense of one's importance, power, knowledge, or identity. It may have a religious, somatic, or other theme.

delusion, persecutory. A delusion in which the central theme is that a person or group is being attacked, harassed, cheated, persecuted, or conspired against. Usually the subject or someone or some group or institution close to him or her is singled out as the object of the persecution.

delusion of reference. A delusion whose theme is that events, objects, or other people in the person's immediate environment have a particular and unusual significance, usually of a negative or pejorative nature. This differs from an idea of reference, in which the false belief is not as firmly held as in a delusion. If the delusion of reference involves a persecutory theme, then a delusion of persecution is present as well. Examples: A woman is convinced that programs on the radio are directed especially at her: when recipes are broadcast, it is to tell her to prepare wholesome food for her child and stop feeding her candy; when dance music is broadcast, it is to tell her to stop what she is doing and start dancing, and perhaps even to resume ballet lessons. A patient notes that the room number of his therapist's office is the same as the number of the hospital room in which his father died and believes that this means there was a plot to kill him.

delusion, somatic. A delusion whose main content pertains to the functioning of one's body. Examples: One's brain is rotting; one is pregnant despite being postmenopausal. Extreme value judgments about the body may, under certain circumstances, already be considered somatic delusions. Example: A person insists that his nose is grossly misshapen despite lack of confirmation of this by observers. Hypochondriacal delusions are also somatic delusions when they involve specific changes in the functioning or structure of the body rather than merely an insistent belief that one has a disease.

delusion, systematized. A single delusion with multiple elaborations or a group of delusions that are all related by the person to a single event or theme. Example: A man who failed his bar examination develops the delusion that this occurred because of a conspiracy involving the university and the bar association. He then attributes all other difficulties in his social and occupational life to this continuing conspiracy.

depersonalization. An alteration in the perception or experience of the self so that the feeling of one's own reality is temporarily lost. This is manifested in a sense of self-estrangement or unreality, which may include the feeling that one's extremities have changed in size, or a sense of seeming to perceive oneself from a distance (usually from above.)

Depersonalization is seen in depersonalization disorder, and may also occur in schizotypal personality disorder and schizophrenia. It is sometimes observed in people without any mental disorder who are experiencing overwhelming anxiety, stress, or fatigue.

depression. Depression is a mood disorder that causes a persistent feeling of sadness and loss of interest. Also called major depressive disorder or clinical depression, it affects how you feel, think and behave and can lead to a variety of emotional and physical problems. You may have trouble doing normal day-to-day activities, and sometimes you may feel as if life isn't worth living. More than just a bout of the blues, depression isn't a weakness and you can't simply "snap out" of it. Depression may require long-term treatment. But don't get discouraged. Most people with depression feel better with medication, psychological counseling or both.[35]

diagnosis. This term refers to the process of identifying specific mental or physical disorders. Some, however, use the term more broadly to refer to a comprehensive

---

[35] "Diseases and Conditions: Depression (Major Depressive Disorder," Mayo Clinic, last modified July 22, 2015, http://www.mayoclinic.org/diseases-conditions/depression/basics/definition/con-20032977.

evaluation that is not limited to identification of specific disorders.

disorientation. Confusion about the date or time of day, where one is (place), or who one is (identity). Disorientation is characteristic of some organic mental disorders, such as delirium and dementia.

distractibility. Attention drawn too frequently to unimportant or irrelevant external stimuli. Example: While being interviewed, a subject's attention is repeatedly drawn to noise from an adjoining office, a book on a shelf, or the interviewer's school ring.

enabling. Enabling refers to the process by which family members, such as partners, parent and children, "enable" an addicted person to continue in their addiction, by failing to set appropriate boundaries, failing to recognize the problem, providing money etc.[36]

evidence-based practice. The integration of the best available research with clinical expertise in the context of patient characteristics, culture and preferences.[37]

flight of ideas. A nearly continuous flow of accelerated speech with abrupt changes from topic to topic, usually based on understandable associations, distracting stimuli, or plays on words. When severe, speech may be disorganized and incoherent. Flight of ideas is most frequently seen in manic episodes, but may also be observed in some cases of organic mental disorders,

---

[36] Elizabeth Hartney, "Definition of Enabling," About Health, last modified June 23, 2014, http://addictions.about.com/od/glossar1/g/defenabling.htm.

[37] "Evidence-Based Practice in Psychology," American Psychological Association, accessed May 3, 2016, http://www.apa.org/practice/resources/evidence/.

schizophrenia, other psychotic disorders, and, occasionally, acute reactions to stress.

formal thought disorder. A disturbance in the form of thought as distinguished from the content of thought. The boundaries of the concept are not clear, and there is no consensus as to which disturbances in speech or thought are included in the concept. For this reason, "formal thought disorder" is not used as a specific descriptive term in DSM-III-R. *See* loosening of associations, incoherence, poverty of content speech, neologisms, blocking, clanging.

generalized anxiety disorder (panic disorder, PTSD, OCD, phobias). Excessive, ongoing anxiety and worry that interfere with day-to-day activities may be a sign of generalized anxiety disorder. It's possible to develop generalized anxiety disorder as a child or an adult. Generalized anxiety disorder has symptoms that are similar to panic disorder, obsessive-compulsive disorder, and other types of anxiety, but they're all different conditions. Living with generalized anxiety disorder can be a long-term challenge. In many cases, it occurs along with other anxiety or mood disorders. In most cases, generalized anxiety disorder improves with medications or talk therapy (psychotherapy). Making lifestyle changes, learning coping skills and using relaxation techniques also can help.[38]

grandiosity. An inflated appraisal of one's worth, power, knowledge, importance, or identity. When extreme,

---

[38] "Diseases and Conditions: Generalized Anxiety Disorder," Mayo Clinic, last modified September 25, 2014, http://www.mayoclinic.org/diseases-conditions/generalized-anxiety-disorder/basics/definition/con-20024562.

grandiosity may be of delusional proportions. Example: A professor who frequently puts his students to sleep with his boring lectures is convinced that he is the most dynamic and exciting teacher at the university.

hallucination. A sensory perception without external stimulation of the relevant sensory organ. A hallucination has the immediate sense of reality of a true perception, although in some instances the source of the hallucination may be perceived as within the body (e.g., an auditory hallucination may be experienced as coming from within the head rather than through the ears). (Some investigators limit the concept of true hallucinations to sensations whose source is perceived as being external to the body, but the clinical significance of this distinction has yet to be demonstrated.

There may or may not be a delusional interpretation of the hallucinatory experience. For example, one person with auditory hallucinations may recognize that he or she is having a false sensory experience, whereas another may be convinced that the source of the sensory experience has an independent physical reality. Strictly speaking, hallucinations indicate a psychotic disturbance only when they are associated with gross impairment in reality testing (*see* psychotic). The term "hallucination," by itself, is not ordinarily applied to the false perceptions that occur during dreaming, while falling asleep (hypnagogic), or when awakening (hypnopompic). Hallucinations occurring in the course of an intensely shared religious experience generally have no pathological significance.

Hallucinations should be distinguished from illusions, in which an external stimulus is misperceived or misinterpreted, and from normal thought processes that are exceptionally vivid. Transient hallucinatory experiences are common in people without mental disorder.

hallucination, auditory. A hallucination of sound, most commonly of voices, but sometimes of clicks, rushing noises, music, etc.

hallucination, gustatory. A hallucination of taste, unpleasant tastes being the most common.

hallucination, olfactory. A hallucination involving smell. Example: A woman complains of a persistent smell of dead bodies. Some people are convinced they have a body odor they themselves cannot smell; this symptom is a delusion, not an olfactory hallucination.

hallucination, somatic. A hallucination involving the perception of a physical experience localized within the body. Example: A feeling of electricity running through one's body. Somatic hallucinations are to be distinguished from unexplained physical sensations; a somatic hallucination can be identified with certainty only when a delusional interpretation of a physical illness is present. A somatic hallucination is to be distinguished also from hypochondriacal preoccupation with, or exaggeration of, normal physical sensations and from a tactile hallucination, in which the sensation is usually related to the skin.

hallucination, tactile. A hallucination involving the sense of touch, often of something on or under the skin. Almost invariably the symptom is associated with a delusional interpretation of the sensation. Examples: A man said he could feel the Devil sticking pins into his flesh; another claimed he could feel himself being penetrated anally; still another complained of experiencing pains, which he attributed to the Devil, throughout his body, although there was no evidence of any physical illness.

A particular tactile hallucination is *formication*, which is the sensation of something creeping or crawling on or under the skin. Often there is a delusional interpretation of the sensation, as when it is attributed to insects or worms. Formication is seen in alcohol withdrawal delirium and the withdrawal phase of cocaine intoxication.

hallucination, visual. A hallucination involving sight, which may consist of formed images, such as people, or of unformed images, such as flashes of light. Visual hallucinations should be distinguished from illusions, which are misperceptions of real external stimuli.

ideas of reference. An idea, held less firmly than a delusion, that events, objects, or other people in the person's immediate environment have a particular and unusual meaning specifically for him or her. *See also* delusion of reference.

identity. The sense of self, providing a unity of personality over time. Prominent disturbances in identity or the sense of self are seen in schizophrenia, borderline personality disorder, and identity disorder.

illogical thinking. Thinking that contains obvious internal contradictions or in which conclusions are reached that are clearly erroneous, given the initial premises. It may be seen in people without mental disorder, particularly in situations in which they are distracted or fatigued. Illogical thinking has psychopathological significance only when it is marked, as in the examples noted below, and when it is not due to cultural or religious values or to an intellectual deficit. Markedly illogical thinking may lead to, or result from, a delusional belief, or may be observed in the absence of delusion.

Examples: A patient explained that she gave her family IBM cards, which she punched, in an effort to improve communication with them. Another patient stated: "Parents are the people that raise you. Parents can be anything—material, vegetable, or mineral—that has taught you something. A person can look at a rock and learn something from it, so a rock is a parent." In response to the question "Why did you go to Kingston?" a patient replied, "Because I believe in the King James Bible and my name is James. I went to Kingston to see the Queen."

illusion. A misperception of a real external stimulus. Examples: The rustling of leaves is heard as the sound of voices; a man claims that when he looks in a mirror, he sees his face distorted and misshapen. *See also* hallucination.

incoherence. Speech that, for the most part, is not understandable, owing to many of the following: a lack of logical or meaningful connection between words, phrases, or sentences; excessive use of incomplete sentences; excessive irrelevancies or abrupt changes in subject matter; idiosyncratic word usage; distorted grammar. Mildly ungrammatical constructions or idiomatic usages characteristic of particular regional or ethnic backgrounds, lack of education, or low intelligence should not be considered incoherence. The term is generally not applied when there is evidence that the disturbance in speech is due to an aphasia.

Example: Interviewer: "Why do you think people believe in God?" Subject: "Um, because making a do in life. Isn't none of that stuff about evolution guiding isn't true anymore now. It all happened a long time ago. It happened in eons and eons and stuff they wouldn't believe in Him. The time that Jesus Christ people believe in their thing people believed in, Jehovah God that they didn't believe in Jesus Christ that much."

Incoherence may be seen in some organic mental disorders, schizophrenia, and other psychotic disorders.

insomnia. Difficulty falling or staying asleep. Initial insomnia is difficulty in falling asleep. Middle insomnia involves an awakening, followed by difficulty returning to sleep, but eventually doing so. Terminal insomnia is awakening at least two hours before one's usual waking time and being unable to return to sleep.

integrated treatment for dual disorders. An approach to treating co-occurring disorders that utilizes one competent treatment team at the same facility to recognize and address all mental health and substance use disorders at the same time. The integrated model of treatment can best be defined by the following seven components:

a. Integration—Both illnesses are seen as primary, and treatment reflects both occurring in the brain at the same time.

b. Comprehensiveness—Treatment includes psychoeducation, individual and group counseling, medication, treatment for medical issues, case management, and family treatment.

c. Assertiveness—Treatment is proactive rather than reactive and includes outreach services.

d. Reduction of negative consequences—The program is client centered and meets the person where they are at rather than meeting the needs of the program. Reducing negative consequences such as homelessness, unemployment, and medical illness is as valued as abstinence and taking medication.

e. Long-term perspective—These are programs that focus on chronic illnesses like heart disease, diabetes, and hypertension and require monitoring and episodes of care throughout life. Programs that can support people in the community and to help integrate them into the community tend to have a long-term perspective.

f. Motivation-based treatment—This treatment finds what the person's goals are and uses those to motivate change. It uses the Stages of Change model to direct treatment interventions.

g. Multiple psychotherapeutic modalities—There is no magic medication that will "cure" these brain diseases. It is vital that treatment includes multiple modalities such as motivational interviewing, cognitive behavioral therapy, exercise, nutrition, self-help, trauma treatment, integrated mental illness, and addiction group and individual counseling.

loosening of associations. Thinking characterized by speech in which ideas shift from one subject to another that is completely unrelated or only obliquely related to the first without the speaker's showing any awareness that the topics are unconnected. Statements that lack a meaningful relationship may be juxtaposed, or the person may shift idiosyncratically from one frame of reference to another. When loosening of associations is severe, speech may be incoherent. The term is generally not applied when abrupt shifts in topics are associated with a nearly continuous flow of accelerated speech (as in flight of ideas).

Examples: Interviewer: "What did you think of the whole Watergate affair?" Subject: "You know I didn't tune in on that, I felt so bad about it. But it seemed to get so murky, and everybody's reports were so negative. Huh, I thought, I don't want any part of this, and I don't care who was in on it, and all I could figure out was Artie had something to do with it. Artie was trying to flush the bathroom toilet of the White House or something. She was trying to do something fairly simple. The tour guests stuck or something. She got blamed because the water overflowed, went down in the basement, down, to the kitchen. They had a, they were going to have to repaint and restore the White House room, the enormous living room. And then it was at this reunion they were having. And it's just such a mess and I just thought, well, I'm just going to pretend like I don't even know what's going on. So I came downstairs 'cause I pretended like I didn't know what was going on, I slipped on the floor of the kitchen, cracking my toe, when I was teaching some kids how to do some double dives."

Loosening of associations may be seen in schizophrenia, manic episodes, and other psychotic disorders.

magical thinking. The person believes his or her thoughts, words, or actions might, or will in some manner, cause or prevent a specific outcome in some way that defies the normal laws of cause and effect. Example: A man believes that if he says a specific prayer three times each night, his mother's death might be prevented indefinably; a mother believes that if she has an angry thought, her child will become ill.

Magical thinking may be part of ideas of reference or may reach delusional proportions when the person maintains a firm conviction about the belief despite evidence to the contrary.

Magical thinking is seen in children, in people in primitive cultures, and in schizotypal personality disorder, schizophrenia, and obsessive-compulsive disorder.

meditate. *Intransitive verb*: (1) To engage in contemplation or reflection. (2) To engage in mental exercise (as concentration on one's breathing or repetition of a mantra) for the purpose of reaching a heightened level of spiritual awareness. *Transitive verb*: (1) To focus one's thoughts on: reflect on or ponder over. (2) To plan or project in the mind.[39]

mental disorder. A significant behavior or psychological syndrome or pattern that occurs in a person and that is associated with present distress (a painful symptom) or disability impairment in one or more important areas of functioning.

mood. A pervasive and sustained emotion that, in the extreme, markedly colors that person's perception of the world. Common examples of mood include depression, elation, anger, and anxiety.

> **mood, dysphoric.** An unpleasant mood, such as depression, anxiety, or irritability.

> **mood, elevated.** A mood that is more cheerful than normal; it does not necessarily imply pathology.

> **mood, euphoric.** An exaggerated feeling of well-being. As a technical term, *euphoric* implies a pathological mood. Whereas the person with a normally elevated mood may describe himself or

---

[39] "Meditate," Merriam-Webster.com, accessed March 3, 2016, http://www.merriam-webster.com/dictionary/meditate.

herself as being in good spirits, very happy, or cheerful, the euphoric person is likely to exclaim that he or she is on top of the world, up in the clouds, or to say, "I feel ecstatic," "I'm flying," or "I am high."

mood, euthymic. Mood in the "normal" range, which implies the absence of depressed or elevated mood.

mood, expansive. Lack of restraint in expressing one's feelings, frequently with an inflated opinion of one's significance or importance. There may also be elevated or euphoric mood.

mood, irritable. Internalized feeling of tension associated with being easily annoyed and provoked to anger.

NAMI Family-to-Family. A free, twelve-session educational program for family, significant others and friends of people living with mental illness. It is a designated evidenced-based program. Research shows that the program significantly improves the coping and problem-solving abilities of the people closest to an individual living with a mental health condition. NAMI Family-to-Family is taught by NAMI-trained family members who have been there, and includes presentations, discussion and interactive exercises.[40]

neologisms. New words invented by the subject, distortions of words, or standard words to which the subject has given new, highly idiosyncratic meanings. The judgment that the subject uses neologisms should be made

---

[40] "NAMI Family-to-Family," National Alliance on Mental Illness, accessed March 3, 2016, https://www.nami.org/Find-Support/NAMI-Programs/NAMI-Family-to-Family.

cautiously and take into account his or her educational and cultural background. Examples: "I was accused of mitigation" (meaning the subject was accused of breaking the law). "They had an insinuating machine next door" (person explaining how her neighbors were bothering her). Neologisms may be observed in schizophrenia and other psychotic disorders.

obsessions. Recurrent, persistent, senseless ideas, thoughts, images, or impulses that are ego-dystonic, that is, they are not experienced as voluntarily produced, but rather as ideas that invade consciousness. Obsessions are characteristic of obsessive-compulsive disorder, and may also be seen in schizophrenia.

orientation. Awareness of where one is in relation to time, place, and person.

panic attacks. Discrete periods of sudden onset of intense apprehension, fearfulness, or terror, often associated with feelings of impending doom. During the attacks there are such symptoms as dyspnea, palpitations, chest pain or discomfort, choking or smothering sensations, and fear of going crazy or losing control. Panic attacks are characteristic of panic disorder, but may also occur in somatization disorder, major depression, and schizophrenia.

paranoid ideation. Ideation, of less than delusional proportions, involving the belief that one is being harassed, persecuted, or unfairly treated. In some instances the term is used when the clinician is unsure of whether the disturbances are actually delusional. Ideas of reference often involve paranoid ideation.

perseveration. Persistent repetition of words, ideas, or subjects so that, once a person begins speaking about a particular subject or uses a particular word, it continually recurs. Perseverations differ from the repetitive use of "stock words" or interjections such as "you know" or "like." Examples: "I think I'll put on my hat, my hat, my hat, my hat." Interviewer: "Tell me what you are like, what kind of person you are." Subject: I'm from Marshalltown, Iowa. That's sixty miles northwest of Des Moines, Iowa. And I'm married at the present time. I'm thirty-six years old. My wife is thirty-five. She lives in Garwin, Iowa. That's fifteen miles southeast of Marshalltown, Iowa. I'm getting a divorce at the present time. And I am at present in a mental institution in Iowa City, Iowa, which is one hundred miles southeast of Marshalltown, Iowa." Perseveration is most commonly seen in organic mental disorders, schizophrenia, and other psychotic disorders.

personality. Deeply ingrained patterns of behavior, which include the way one relates to, perceives, and thinks about the environment and oneself. Personality *traits* are prominent aspects of personality, and do not imply pathology. Personality *disorder* implies inflexible and maladaptive patterns of sufficient severity to cause either significant impairment in adaptive functioning or subjective distress.

phobia. A persistent, irrational fear of a specific object, activity, or situation that results in a compelling desire to avoid the dreaded object, activity, or situation (the phobic stimulus). More commonly, the person does actually avoid the feared situation or object, though he or she recognizes that the fear is unreasonable and unwarranted by the actual dangerousness of the object, activity, or situation. Some people with a phobia claim that their avoidance is rational because they anticipate overwhelming anxiety or some other strong emotion that is out of their control; they do not claim, however, that their anxiety is rationally justified.

poverty of content of speech. Speech that is adequate in amount but conveys little information because of vagueness, empty repetitions, or use of stereotyped or obscure phrases. The interviewer may observe that the person has spoken at some length but has not given adequate information to answer a question. Alternatively, the person may also provide enough information to answer the question, but requires many words to do so, so that his or her lengthy reply can be summarized in a sentence or two. The expression *poverty of content of speech* is generally not used when the speech is, for the most part, not understandable (incoherence). Example: Interviewer: "Okay. Why is it, do you think, that people believe in God?" Patient: "Well, first of all because, He is the person that, is their personal savior. He walks with me and talks with me. And uh, the understanding that I have, a lot of peoples, they don't really know their own personal self. Because they ain't, they all, just don't know their own personal self. They don't know that He uh, seemed like to me, a lot of 'em don't understand that He walks and talks with them. And uh, show 'em their way to go. I understand also that, every man and every lady, is just not pointed in the same direction. Some are pointed different. They go in their different ways. The way that Jesus Christ wanted 'em to go. Myself, I am pointed in the ways of uh, knowing right from wrong and doing it. I can't do any more, or not less than that."

poverty of speech. Restriction in the amount of speech, so that spontaneous speech and replies to questions are brief and unelaborated. When the condition is severe, replies may be monosyllabic, and some questions may be unanswered. Poverty of speech occurs frequently in schizophrenia, major depressive episodes, and organic mental disorders, such as dementia.

pressure of speech. Speech that is increased in amount, accelerated, and difficult or impossible to interrupt. Usually it is also loud and emphatic. Frequently the person talks without any social stimulation, and may continue to talk even though no one is listening. Pressure of speech is most often seen in manic episodes, but may also occur in some cases of organic mental disorders, major depression with psychomotor agitation, schizophrenia, other psychotic disorders, and, occasionally, acute reactions to stress.

prodromal. Early signs or symptoms of a disorder.

pseudodementia. Clinical features resembling a dementia that are not due to organic brain dysfunction or disease. Pseudodementia may occur in a major depressive episode or may be seen in factitious disorder with psychological symptoms.

psychomotor agitation. Excessive motor activity associated with a feeling of inner tension; the activity is usually nonproductive and repetitious. When the agitation is severe, it may be accompanied by shouting or loud complaining. The term should be used in a technical sense to refer only to states of tension or restlessness that are accompanied by observable excessive motor activity. Examples: inability to sit still, pacing, wringing of hands, pulling at clothes.

psychomotor retardation. Visible, generalized slowing down of physical reactions, movements, and speech.

psycho-social-educational-spiritual therapy. A form of individual or group counseling that provides comprehensive treatment that includes psychological treatment, education, community integration, spiritual interventions, and guidance to people with addiction and their families.

psychotic. Gross impairment of reality testing and the creation of a new reality. The term may be used to describe a person at a given time, or a mental disorder in which, at some time during its course, all people with the disorder are psychotic. When a person is psychotic, he or she incorrectly evaluates the accuracy of his or her perceptions and thoughts and makes incorrect inferences about external reality, even in the face of contrary evidence. The term "psychotic" does not apply to minor distortions of reality that involve matters of relative judgment. For example, a depressed person who underestimates his achievements would not be described as psychotic, whereas one who believes he has caused a natural catastrophe would be so described. Direct evidence of psychotic behavior is the presence of either delusions or hallucinations (without insight into their pathological nature). The term "psychotic" is sometimes appropriate when a person's behavior is so grossly disorganized that a reasonable inference can be made that reality testing is markedly disturbed. Examples include markedly incoherent speech without apparent awareness by the person that the speech is not understandable, and the agitated, inattentive, and disoriented behavior seen in alcohol withdrawal delirium.

residual. The phase of an illness that occurs after remission of the florid symptoms or the full syndrome. Examples: The residual states of autistic disorder, attention-deficit/hyperactivity disorder, and schizophrenia.

schizoaffective disorder. Schizoaffective disorder is a condition in which a person experiences a combination of schizophrenia symptoms—such as hallucinations or delusions—and mood disorder symptoms, such as mania or depression. Schizoaffective disorder is not as well understood or well defined as other mental health conditions. This is largely because schizoaffective disorder is a mix of mental health conditions—including schizophrenic and mood disorder features—that may run a unique course in each affected person. Untreated, people with schizoaffective disorder may lead lonely lives and have trouble holding down a job or attending school. Or, they may rely heavily on family or live in supported living environments, such as group homes. Treatment can help manage symptoms and improve the quality of life for people with schizoaffective disorder.[41]

schizophrenia. Schizophrenia is a severe brain disorder in which people interpret reality abnormally. Schizophrenia may result in some combination of hallucinations, delusions, and extremely disordered thinking and behavior. Contrary to popular belief, schizophrenia isn't a split personality or multiple personality. The word "schizophrenia" does mean "split mind," but it refers to a disruption of the usual balance of emotions and thinking. Schizophrenia is a chronic condition, usually requiring lifelong treatment.[42]

schizophrenogenic mother. Stereotypical mother figure for an individual exhibiting schizophrenia, generally described as cold, rejecting, emotionally disturbed, perfectionist, domineering, and lacking in sensitivity. Conversely, she is also described as being overprotective, encouraging dependence, and both rigidly moral and seductive. Held to play a causal role in schizophrenic development, this view has become outdated.[43]

severe and persistent mental illness. Every state is different in its definition of this term, but it is agreed upon

[41] "Diseases and Conditions: Schizoaffective Disorder," Mayo Clinic, last modified January 25, 2014, http://www.mayoclinic.org/diseases-conditions/schizoaffective-disorder/basics/definition/con-20029221.

[42] "Diseases and Conditions: Schizophrenia," Mayo Clinic, last modified January 24, 2014, http://www.mayoclinic.org/diseases-conditions/schizophrenia/basics/definition/con-20021077.

[43] Pam MS, "What Is Schizophrenogenic Mother?" Psychology Dictionary, accessed March 3, 2016, http://psychologydictionary.org/schizophrenogenic-mother/.

that this usually refers to an adult with a serious mental illness and usually includes major depression, anxiety disorders, PTSD, bipolar disorder, schizophrenia, schizoaffective disorder, and obsessive-compulsive disorder.

sign. An objective manifestation of a pathological condition. Signs are observed by the examiner rather than reported by the individual.

symptom. A manifestation of a pathological condition. Although in some uses of the term it is limited to subjective complaints, in common use "symptom" includes objective signs of pathological conditions as well.

syndrome. A group of symptoms that occur together and that constitute a recognizable condition. "Syndrome" is less specific that "disorder" or "disease." The term "disease" generally implies a specific etiology or pathophysiologic process. In DSM-III-R most of the disorders are, in fact, syndromes.

Mary Ryan Woods is a licensed registered nurse and a licensed alcohol and drug abuse counselor with more than thirty years of experience in substance abuse services and community mental health programs. Mary created WestBridge in 2001 and continues to serve as chief executive officer of the organization.

WestBridge is a private non-profit organization dedicated to supporting the recovery of families and individuals who experience co-occurring mental illness and substance use disorders. With programs in Manchester, New Hampshire; Medford, Massachusetts; and Brooksville, Florida, WestBridge uses evidence-based practices to provide integrated dual diagnosis treatment for adult men and women.

Mary received her nursing diploma from St. Joseph's Hospital School of Nursing in Elmira, New York, and her master's degree in Human Service Administration from Springfield College in Springfield, Massachusetts. Among other professional experiences and appointments, she has taught Introduction to Addictions at the University of New Hampshire and was president of the National Association of Alcoholism and Drug Abuse Counselors (NAADAC).

Adrienne Murray is a Project Manager with Dunleavy & Associates, a Philadelphia-based professional services firm that provides project management, contracted leadership, and advisory services to non-profit organizations. Adrienne has a background in social work and collaborates with WestBridge in a variety of capacities. While Adrienne loves her work as a consultant, she most treasures her role as wife and mother. She makes her home in the suburbs of Philadelphia with her husband and their five children.

100% of the sale proceeds from this book will go to the WestBridge Recovery Opportunity Fund.

This fund provides treatment scholarships to WestBridge participants and families in need of support for continuing care.

35377430R00083

Made in the USA
Middletown, DE
30 September 2016